SELF THE HIDDEN IDOL

To Gaochoua Vue

May The lord Jesus bless You

William R. Seal

2 Cor. 5:17

SELF THE HIDDEN IDOL

Willie R. Smith

ELM HILL

A Division of
HarperCollins Christian Publishing

www.elmhillbooks.com

Self The Hidden Idol

Published in Nashville, Tennessee, by Elm Hill, an imprint of Thomas Nelson. Elm Hill and Thomas Nelson are registered trademarks of HarperCollins Christian Publishing, Inc.

Scripture quotations marked CJB are taken from the Complete Jewish Bible by David H. Stern. Copyright © 1998. All rights reserved. Used by permission of Messianic Jewish Publishers, 6120 Day Long Lane, Clarksville, MD 21029. www.messianicjewish.net.

Scripture quotations marked ESV are from the ESV˚ Bible (The Holy Bible, English Standard Version˚). Copyright © 2001 by Crossway, a publishing ministry of Good News Publishers. Used by permission. All rights reserved.

Scripture quotations marked KJV are from the King James Version. Public domain.

Scripture quotations marked NASB are from New American Standard Bible˚. Copyright © 1960, 1962, 1963, 1968, 1971, 1972, 1973, 1975, 1977, 1995 by The Lockman Foundation. Used by permission. (www.Lockman.org)

Scripture quotations marked NIV are from the Holy Bible, New International Version˚, NIV˚. Copyright © 1973, 1978, 1984, 2011 by Biblica, Inc.˚ Used by permission of Zondervan. All rights reserved worldwide. www.Zondervan.com. The "NIV" and "New International Version" are trademarks registered in the United States Patent and Trademark Office by Biblica, Inc.˚

Scripture quotations marked NKJV are from the New King James Version˚. © 1982 by Thomas Nelson. Used by permission. All rights reserved.

Scripture quotations marked THE MESSAGE are from *The Message*. Copyright © by Eugene H. Peterson 1993, 1994, 1995, 1996, 2000, 2001, 2002. Used by permission of NavPress. All rights reserved. Represented by Tyndale House Publishers, Inc.

Library of Congress Cataloging-in-Publication Data

Library of Congress Control Number: 2019921041

ISBN 978-1-400330126 (Paperback)
ISBN 978-1-400330133 (eBook)

TABLE OF CONTENTS

Acknowledgments   ix
Editorial Thanks   xi

Section 1. Laying the Foundation

Chapter 1. The Decision   2
Chapter 2. The Purchase   10
Chapter 3. The Changed Mindset   17
Chapter 4. The Needs   22

Section 2. The Idol

Chapter 5. The Hidden Idol   30
Chapter 6. The Heart   41
Chapter 7. The Soul   51
Chapter 8. The Strength   57
Chapter 9. The Mind   62

Section 3. This is Living

Chapter 10. The Strength to Do!   70
Chapter 11. The Denial   75

Section 4. Faith In Action

Chapter 12. Love Your Neighbor as Yourself 82

Chapter 13. Good Intentions, But Not God's Will 90

Chapter 14. Seeing God in and Through Your Circumstances 97

Chapter 15. The Healing 104

Epilogue. No More Excuses! 111

Supplemental Reading "A" 117

Supplemental Reading "B" 121

Forward

The inspiration for writing this book comes at an important point in history, one in which the effects and consequences of our digression from Truth are severely felt, yet increasingly ignored. The times we live in now are akin to Paul's warning in 2 Timothy 4:3, "For the time is coming when people will not endure sound teachings, but having itching ears they will accumulate for themselves teachers to suit their own passions." Every day we see the direct effects of a world that has turned completely from God and turned completely inward: violence, corruption, greed, adultery, envy, and everything in between. On both a macro- and microscopic level, these are the direct results of humanity's attempt to place ourselves in the center of the universe, to fully assert ourselves as god.

And we are failing miserably.

Still, we press on unperturbed day after day, falling further and further away from God, even establishing systems and ordinances that hasten our falling as a community, all in the name of "doing what's best for me" or "living my best life." That is why this book is so important. In order to move forward, we must first take a step back and rediscover the foundation of who we are in Christ. We must realize how far we've fallen away and come back to God – and thankfully, no distance is too great for God's grace and redemption.

The author of this book, Willie Smith, is not some highly educated writer who intends to confuse you with Christian jargon and deep theology. He is not a world-renowned author, nor does he have any prior experience in writing. No, Willie is merely a common man, but he is foremost an obedient servant of God. We have seen firsthand Willie's complete subjugation to the righteousness of God, as well as his humility to serve at any time anywhere in the community around him. He does not fear truth, nor does he fear man, for his life is totally led and protected by the Holy Spirit who guides him. Indeed, although Willie's hands labored at the words on these pages, it is God who writes this book through him. Every word in it comes from God and Willie has only written what the Holy Spirit has pressed upon his heart – nothing more, nothing less. With little regard to how pleasing or fancy the words may sound, he has lovingly poured God's truth into these pages, all for the sole purpose of turning this generation's attention and worship away from the mirror, back to the one and only God Almighty.

The Bible says in Matthew 5:16 that when the world sees our deeds as Christians, they shall know that we are His children. In Willie, we see attributes of the apostle Paul's passion to preach the salvation, love, and grace of Jesus Christ. Willie often likes to ask the question, "Are we better than Jesus?" And while we know the answer to that question is a resounding "NO," the actions of the world, and sadly even those of the body of Christ, would suggest otherwise. We challenge you as a reader to discover the truth for yourself as you take your time and make your way through these pages. Have your Bible close at hand, and be ready to answer the questions, "Is this true? Does it align with God's Word?" If it does, and we know that it does, we urge you to allow God's truth to transform your attitude, actions, and outlook on life..

Forward written by Shengxi Smith (Wife)
and Hannah Townend (Daughter)

ACKNOWLEDGMENTS

I am most thankful to God for this wonderful opportunity. To think about my life and all that I have been through, I am humbled by His Grace toward me. The words in Paul's letter to Timothy sum it up best:

> I thank Christ Jesus our Lord, who has strengthened me, because He considered me faithful, putting me into service, even though I was formerly a blasphemer and a persecutor and a violent aggressor. Yet I was shown mercy because I acted ignorantly in unbelief.
> (1 TIMOTHY 1:12–13 NASB)

God revealing His son Jesus to me and then putting me in service to make disciples has truly been special to me. Each and every time I think about this, it causes me to be even more humbled and more thankful for His Love and Life that live in me.

I am also very thankful for my lovely wife, Shengxi. She has always been very supportive and understanding through the process of living this lifestyle that most would call "abnormal," a lifestyle of trusting God with all that we are and all that we have. She understands the importance of sharing the Gospel and the time that is involved in making disciples. God has truly blessed me with my lovely wife, Shengxi.

My two daughters, Hannah and Halle—these two girls have meant so much to me over the years. They have seen me through all the ups and downs in my life, yet we have always been there for each other. In the early years, we would sit around the table, and whenever God taught me something, I would pull out the big Post-it note and teach it to them to see if it made sense; poor girls had to sit through and listen to a lot back then, and I continue to be truly blessed by them and their love and support.

Special thanks to all my family and friends that God has blessed me with over the years. There are too many to name, but I am thankful for each and every one of them, especially my seven sisters and my late mother and father, for they all are very important to me. Your love and support over the years have meant so much to me.

Thanks to all the ministers and church families—they have all had an impact on my life and helped me in my understanding and walk with God. A special thanks to my good friend James Gilbert—he has always been there for me no matter what I have gone through in life and he has always offered godly wisdom and many days of long conversations.

May God bless you as you read *Self: The Hidden Idol*.

EDITORIAL THANKS

Special thanks to Brentwood and Hannah Townend. The time that you put in helping edit this book means so much to me. Thank you for serving the Lord through your gifting.

EXPLANATIONS

As you begin to read this book, you'll notice that I often quote from the *Complete Jewish Bible* (CJB) as my main source of Scripture though I also employ several other versions to help illustrate some points. I highly encourage you to have your Bible close at hand while reading to study the Scriptures for yourself. I pray the Holy Spirit may enlighten you to the truth within God's Word. Below, I have included various definitions and explanations of terms and ideas used throughout this book.

Human Needs: These are the basic human needs as shown in Genesis before the fall. These needs, and how we go about ensuring they are met, are an indicator of who we worship.

1. **Creator**: the need for a superior being, for a Father

In the beginning, God created the heavens and the earth.

(GENESIS 1:1 CJB)

2. **Provision**: to be supported with housing, clothing, food, supplies, nurturing, and so on

And God said, "Behold, I have given you every plant yielding seed that is on the face of all the earth, and every tree with seed in its fruit. You shall have them for food."

(GENESIS 1:29 ESV)

3. **Procreation**: to keep life going, to reproduce in our likeness, sexual desires and so on

And God blessed them. And God said to them, "Be fruitful and multiply and fill the earth."

(GENESIS 1:28A ESV)

4. **Responsibility**: responsibility, reliability, and labor

The LORD God took the man and put him in the garden of Eden to work it and keep it.

(GENESIS 2:15 ESV)

5. **Authority**: to have power, dominion, management

...subdue it and have dominion over the fish of the sea and over the birds of the heavens and over every living thing that moves on the earth.

(GENESIS 1:28B ESV)

6. **Purpose**: a reason for life, hope, destination, meaning, design, mission

Then the LORD God formed the man of dust from the ground and breathed into his nostrils the breath of life, and the man became a living creature.

(GENESIS 2:7 ESV)

7. **Companionship**: to be in community or relationship, to serve as a funnel for God's love, harmony, familiarity, and friendship

Then the LORD God said, "It is not good that the man should be alone; I will make him a helper fit for him."

(GENESIS 2:18 ESV)

8. **Rest**: a time of recuperation, stillness, and silence

And on the seventh day God finished his work that he had done, and he rested on the seventh day from all his work that he had done.

(GENESIS 2:2 ESV)

9. **Order**: some form of guidance, direction, instruction

And the LORD God commanded the man, saying, "You may surely eat of every tree of the garden, but of the tree of the knowledge of good and evil you shall not eat, for in the day that you eat of it you shall surely die."

(GENESIS 2:16–17 ESV)

10. **Purity**: approval, acceptance, innocence, to be without defect

And the man and his wife were both naked and were not ashamed.

(GENESIS 2:25 ESV)

11. **A Source of Life**: to know from whom we derive our identity

…including the tree of life [Christ/Holy Spirit] in the middle of the garden, as well as the tree of the knowledge of good and evil (Sin/Satan).

(GENESIS 2:9B CJB)

Jewish Bible terms defined:

- Adonai: Lord, Lord God, My Lord
- Yeshua: Hebrew name for Jesus
- Messiah: Hebrew name for Christ
- Stake: the Cross of Christ

Self: comprised of spirit, soul, and body; it is who we are and our desire to provide for our needs as listed above. The needs are the same for both the believer and the unbeliever

Sin: to miss the mark. Sin is a source of life that is always in direct opposition to God, that is, Satan, who will always choose to miss the mark, that being God!

Sins: for the believer, it is to listen to the voice of Sin (Satan) and to act or live independently of God; for the unbeliever, it is their natural desire

> Indeed, we all once lived this way—we followed the passions of our old nature and obeyed the wishes of our old nature and our own thoughts. In our natural condition we were headed for God's wrath, just like everyone else.
>
> **(EPHESIANS 2:3 CJB)**

Temptation: Satan's method of deceiving the believer into thinking that God will not meet his needs (purity, companionship, purpose, provision, etc.) and that he must trust a source (Sin/Satan/Self) other than God!

> Rather, each person is being tempted whenever he is being dragged off and enticed by the bait of his own desire.
>
> **(JAMES 1:14 CJB)**

Old Nature: the life into which we were born with Sin as the source; a life derived from Adam, where the seed of Sin lives, which manifests itself through sins in the unbeliever's life. The passions and desires of the old nature are completely incompatible with God and will always seek to live in opposition of God. Sin is the source of how the old nature meets its needs

> You are of your father the devil, and you want to do the desires of your father.
>
> **(JOHN 8:44)**

> …the one who practices sin is of the devil; for the devil has sinned from the beginning.
>
> **(1 JOHN 3:8)**

New Nature: the new life to which we were raised when we put our faith in Christ. As a New Creation, Jesus is now the source of life in the believer by the indwelling life of the Holy Spirit. Our same human needs are now met through their rightful creator, Jesus Christ.

> Therefore, if anyone is united with the Messiah (The Christ), he is a new creation—the old has passed; look, what has come is fresh and new!
>
> **(2 COR 5:17 CJB)**

> You will recognize them by their fruit. Can people pick grapes from thorn bushes, or figs from thistles? Likewise, every healthy tree produces good fruit, but a poor tree produces bad fruit. A healthy tree cannot bear bad fruit, or a poor tree good fruit. Any tree that does not produce good fruit is cut down and thrown in the fire!
>
> **(MATTHEW 7:17-19 CJB)**

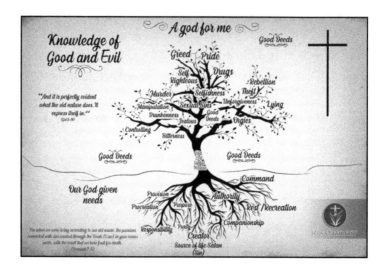

In summary, every human being is born with God-given needs. Through the Fall, Adam and Eve chose to become slaves to Sin (Satan) as their source of life (John 8:44). Because of this choice, it impacted everyone born after them and we are all born sinners. "Here is how it works: it was through one individual that sin entered the world, and through sin, death; and in this way death passed through to the whole human race, inasmuch as everyone sinned"

(**Romans 5:12 CJB**)

As the needs mentioned earlier arise in our life, the source (sin) teaches us ways to get these needs met independently of God. This life will even produce some good moral deeds, as well as some evil deeds, but ultimately, it is still the wrong source.

The Cross of Christ solved the problem that man had, killing off the old evil nature, along with its passion and desires, and freeing us to become one with Christ. As we receive Christ into our hearts, we are connected to the true righteous source, Jesus, who bears fruit of Righteousness in our lives.

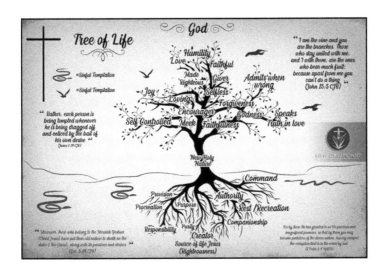

Even though we are made righteous and Christ's life is now flowing in and through us, Satan's temptation still tries to present us with external solutions to meet internal needs. The more we fix our thoughts on our human needs instead of the source, we will find ourselves, as Paul stated, "wasting your time thinking about how to provide for the sinful desires of your old nature"

(ROMANS 13:14)

The key to victory over this life is Christ Jesus as our life, looking to the one who created us with these needs and who is the only one who can truly meet them. Let us now dive into *Self: The Hidden Idol*!

PREFACE

I can remember when I was a child watching this cartoon show where the shadow was doing the opposite of what the object was doing. I thought to myself how crazy that was, but for some time, I found myself checking my own shadow to see if it would do the opposite of what I was doing. To no surprise, it was always copying me; whatever I did my shadow did also. My shadow did not have a mind of its own—it only did what I did. If I raised my hand, the shadow of my hand was raised. If I walked, my shadow would move also. My shadow was my shadow.

> *…and they were saying to the woman, 'It is no longer because of what you said that we believe, for we have heard for ourselves and know that this One is indeed the Savior of the world.'*
>
> **(JOHN 4:42 NASB)**

We are all familiar with the story of the woman at the well. Maybe it was a story you heard in Sunday school and it just stuck with you because it was the first story you ever read in the Bible. The story may have challenged you to go beyond your cultural boundaries because Jesus spoke to a Samaritan woman, or maybe you became inspired by the power of sharing the Gospel because the Samaritan woman heard from Jesus and shared what she heard with men— and they believed! There may be several reasons why this story stands out to you, but I would like to focus specifically on the last verse of the story.

After Jesus had stayed with the Samaritans for a while, their belief that had initially come from the Samaritan woman's testimony transformed. They were no longer basing their belief solely upon what the woman had said or from the woman's life experience. The woman's testimony got them wanting a taste of Jesus, but they ultimately came to believe because they were able to experience and hear Jesus' words for themselves. After spending time with Jesus, they realized that the Samaritan woman was only the shadow, or a voice to the Truth, and were brought into the wonderful revelation that Jesus was the object (the Savior of the World), just as the woman had come to know Him.

This is what Jesus had in mind when He died on the cross and was raised from the dead that upon believing in Him, He would give us a new Life (His Life). His death and resurrection allows us to live in perfect union with Him, hearing His words spoken to us moment by moment as we experience His life through us. John 14:20 and 15:4 paints the picture of how we abide in Christ and He in us, the perfect union between Christ and man. Abiding in Christ means no longer living in the shadows of what others have said and what they have experienced. We can now experience Christ for ourselves!

The shadow does not act on its own volition; it only does what the object does. Jesus said it best in John 15:19: "I only do that what I see my Father doing, I do not act on my own accord." Of the Holy Spirit, Jesus said in John 16:13, He would not speak on His own accord but only what He hears from the Father. The Holy Trinity—the Father, the Son, and the Holy Spirit—always operated as one!

As parents and leaders at work, in community, church, or wherever God has us, we are not to be the source or the answer for life. Instead, we are to allow Christ Himself to be the answer through us. Too often we put ourselves as the source, as the one in whom people should trust for their hope, and in some cases, we do this without even knowing it. We find ourselves wanting people to come to us for information and direction, but in doing so, we fail to point people to Christ as their true source of life. There should only be one source in our lives, and that is Jesus Christ Himself; that was made clear when He said in John 14:6, "I am The Way, The Truth and The Life." He has graciously equipped us with His life and we are directed to point people to Christ. We are to come alongside and bear one another's burdens as we help people realign their focus on Christ. When we begin to think we are the source for people and their problems, however, we are setting ourselves up as god, and even without our realizing it, we indirectly start desiring praise for our knowledge or accomplishments.

I noticed this in my own life while raising my two daughters. As they grew, I took the time to teach them about God, what Christ did for us, and how the Holy Spirit was given to them to empower them to live the Christian life. As I continued to teach them and they got older, without even knowing it, I was beginning to desire to be the source of information for my girls. I wanted them to learn from me and to know that I had the answers. I was putting myself on a pedestal as an idol to them.

Then one day, God pressed upon my heart to share one of my failures with them. I couldn't believe God was asking me to do this—the idea of potentially tainting the perfect image they had of me was terrifying. Despite that doubt, I said yes to God and did as He commanded because I had to remove my shadow so that they could see the true object of their faith. I confessed to them the sins I had been dealing with at that time. As I shared my failure with them, at first I felt like I had let my girls down, but God quickly showed me that I had really shared my life genuinely with them and that it helped them to live. What I really did was tear down their idol—me. This taught them that their earthly father was not perfect but that together we would put our trust in our Heavenly Father and Him alone. There is only one person that they need to put their trust in, and that is Christ. He is the only one who is able to save, and He is the one who will never let them down. Through that vulnerable moment of sharing with my children, our trust in God deepened and our familial relationship grew stronger. They no longer saw me as the superhero, and I no longer needed to be the superhero. They saw that we altogether needed to wholly trust God.

*You may be that person who wants to be the source for people in your circle and their problems. You may feel as though you have to be strong and never show weaknesses. You may think you have to be perfect in everything you say and do, never showing your failures. You may feel as if you've always had to give the right answer or have the correct solutions to everybody's problems. This will only weigh you down, leaving you with a burden so heavy that giving up may feel like the only solution. Know this: Jesus Christ already carried that burden on the cross! Allow Him to not only be the source in your life, but the source to those He has entrusted you to as well; in this our Father in Heaven is glorified. We are but messengers as we reflect Christ to the world we live in. It is **okay** to be the **shadow** and not be the object—**the shadow of Christ**—for in Him we live and have our beings*

(ACTS 17:28)

Take a moment and think about your own relationship with Christ. Are you someone who only reflects or repeats what you have heard someone else say? Are you basing your belief solely on someone else's experience? There is nothing wrong with this as one grows in their walk with Christ, but Christ wants to have His own intimate personal relationship with you where you talk and experience Him for yourself daily. If you feel that you are living as a shadow of someone else other than Christ, then it is time to place your trust in God to change the way you are thinking. Start by thanking God for any people who have shared their experiences from their respective relationship with Christ with you. Next, thank God that He wants to talk to you and wants you to experience His life flowing through you. This is a faith transaction. Colossians 2:6 states, "just as you received Him (Christ) so walk in Him." How did we receive Him? According to Ephesians 2:8, it was by Grace through faith!

Now take time to enjoy this sweet lovely union with Christ, for He paid a great price for us to be able to enjoy Him! He paid the ultimate penalty for our sins with His life, but He now lives so that we can also live in a beautiful relationship with our Heavenly Father.

May we say with the Samaritans: "It is no longer because of what you said that we believe, for we have heard for ourselves and know that this One is indeed the Savior of the world."

LAYING THE FOUNDATION

CHAPTER 1

THE DECISION

Therefore, if anyone is united with the Messiah (Christ), he is a new creation—the old has passed; look, what has come is fresh and new! And it is all from God, who through the Messiah (Christ) has reconciled us to himself and has given us the work of that reconciliation.

(2 CORINTHIANS 5:17–18 CJB)

B efore we investigate the hidden idol of "self," we must first face the reality of what Scripture has to say about us. We can't properly look at the idol of self if we don't know who we are in relation to Christ. Without this knowledge, our eyes will never be opened to the hidden idol. In the eyes of the Almighty God, there are only two camps you can belong to— either you have confessed Jesus Christ as your Lord and Savior and have been admitted into the Book of Life or you are yet to come to know Christ and classified as a sinner. Your ability to understand, comprehend, and heed what is written in this little book depends greatly on which side you're on.

For my fellow brothers and sisters in Christ, we who have confessed Christ as our Lord and Savior are no longer slaves to the old, evil nature into which we were born! Indeed, the old nature is dead! If you have put your faith in Christ, your former sinful self was crucified on the cross with Christ. A full status change occurred when we placed our faith in Christ, and our name was changed from sinner to saint **(Romans 6:6, Galatians 2:20)**.

Our blind wandering was turned to a clear sight of God, shown through His son Jesus. He did more than just "fix" us when we became saved. He threw off the old nature once and for all and raised us to a new life! This literal and spiritual death was required so that we could be born again instead of staying in Satan's family (as he is the father of sin **(John 8:44)**); we are born again into the body of Christ, brought forth through the life of Jesus **(Romans 6:4, Colossians 2:12)**.

This is not only something that we can look forward to when we die and go to heaven; it is also true of us today. Dear Christian, your old evil self is just as dead and powerless as the bodies that lie dormant in any graveyard. It does not exist anymore. We are now to believe and live by faith in our new identity!

Now, it's one thing to proclaim this truth, but it's another to live it out every day. Despite the fact that we know we are made new in Christ, we don't always feel that way. We are permanently made righteous forever, yet sometimes we don't feel righteous. We are New Creations, yet we still fall short at times and revert to the habits of the old nature.

How could this be?

In Romans, Paul instructed us to:

...clothe yourselves with the Lord Yeshua the Messiah (Jesus Christ); and don't waste your time thinking about how to provide for the sinful desires of your old nature.

(ROMANS 13:14 CJB)

Instead of fixing our eyes on the truth of Jesus' life residing in us, we've bought into the lie that Satan tells us, the lie that we are still sinners and that we are saved by grace but still broken at heart. Satan's tricks haven't changed; he uses the same tactics today that he employed on Adam and Eve in the garden. His goal is to deceive us into thinking that God is holding back from us and that God has kept this new life from our reach. Far too often, people believe the lie that the old nature, created in Adam, is still able to command how we live.

We oftentimes become so obsessed with beauty, power, intelligence, and status that we seek to bring honor and glory through those things onto ourselves rather than God. This lie is reminiscent of the father of lies, Satan. In Ezekiel, we see a brief description of the fall of Satan and his conceited nature: "Your heart was proud because of your beauty; you corrupted your wisdom for the sake of your splendor" **(Ezekiel 28:17a)**. Satan looked to himself, rather than to the one who created him, and it caused him to fall away from God. This, too, is the very thing that the serpent did with Eve, essentially whispering, "Look at who you are… you can be so much more! But only if you do this one thing—trust yourself and not the one who created you." Sinful self always looks out for self. It constantly seeks to satisfy itself first and to maintain its status as the highest priority in our lives.

We've become more focused on trying to figure out ways to make provisions for our old, dead, and sinful ways of life. Like a dog returning to its own vomit, we try to revive our old habits and fit them into our new life in Christ. We chase after the world's version of sex, love, money, and so on when God has so lovingly called us to something greater!

We certainly won't always *feel* like New Creations because emotions shift and drift like the wind, but no matter what, we must trust in what God has said about who we are in Christ. The time has come for us to stop making way for the old evil nature (seeking to get our needs meet independently of God) and live out of our new nature. As we live according to our new self, Christ as our life, our actions will be more in line of a dependent life in God just as Jesus lived.

No matter how hard Satan tries to get us to believe the lie, we must make a strong decision to meditate on what God has said in His word. I urge you now, make a conscious decision to take time and ruminate on the truth mentioned in the Scriptures above and pray through them. Let the Holy Spirit lead you into all truth! These may be Scriptures that you already know by heart, but now I encourage, nay, I challenge you to meditate further on these Scriptures. Consider where you may be in your walk with Christ, as this is a reality that does not fit into human, earthly logic.

Maybe you've wandered away from the faith or decided to engage in sinful behavior or maybe you have fully embraced the customs of this world over those of the Word of God. If we are honest, all of us have been there at one or even several points in our walk, but God has commanded us to turn from our wicked ways, return to Him, and seek Him. In the Book of Revelation, He instructs:

> *Therefore, remember where you were before you fell, turn from this sin, and do what you used to do before.*
>
> **(REVELATION 2:5A CJB)**

Now allow the Lord to refresh you in your walk with Him that you may return to the joy of the Lord as your strength and the source of your life.

Let's stop making provisions for the lusts of the old nature, getting our human needs meet independently of God. It never has and never will bring about anything good or pleasing to God. Let us even rid ourselves of thoughts or comments that suggest that the old nature is alive again. **Galatians 5:24** explains that we have put our old nature, along with its passions and desires, to *death*. Where is the excuse now? Please don't try to find one, just let the truth of God's Word be a light unto your path in life. Start walking in the victory that Jesus has paid for you to have for eternity!

> *Those who keep sowing in the field of their old nature (trying to get our human needs met independently of God), in order to meet its demands, will eventually reap ruin; but those who keep sowing in the field of the Spirit will reap from the Spirit everlasting life.*
>
> **(GALATIANS 6:8 CJB)**

What About Everyone Else?

For those who have either rejected Christ or have not yet put their faith in Him, the old nature is not yet dead. It is still very much alive, dictating your very thoughts and actions. This is true of those who have not repented of their sins and have not accepted Jesus as their Lord and Savior. Every human on this earth started at this point in life, but because of Jesus Christ, none of us is eternally confined to this plight.

For those who do not know, Jesus Christ, the one and only begotten son of God, came down from His high position in heaven to selflessly sacrifice His body for the atonement of our sins. He offered Himself up to be crucified by the very people who were entrusted with His word; then He rose again on the third day, thereby conquering death and making way for us to be reconciled with God. It is because of Jesus' selflessness and obedience to God's will that we now have the option to partake in eternal life. For John wrote,

I have written you these things so that you may know that you have eternal life—you who keep trusting in the person and power of the Son of God.

(1 JOHN 5:13 CJB)

Just as John wanted the church to know, I, too, want you to know without a shadow of a doubt that you are signed and sealed for eternity. It's not enough to guess at the state of your eternal salvation—this is the most important choice you will make in this life on Earth. If you have not yet put your faith in Christ or are simply unsure about where you stand, this moment is the perfect time for you to stop and pray, confess that you are a sinner, repent from that former way of life, and call upon the Lord Jesus to save you, for we know that without faith, it is impossible to please God, for it is written:

…whoever approaches him must trust that he does exist and that he becomes a Rewarder to those who seek him out.

(HEBREWS 11:6 CJB)

Here is a sample prayer that you can pray to invite Jesus to come and live His life through you:

"Who do you say I am?"
God, thank you for making your Son, Jesus, known to me. I confess that Jesus is the Messiah, the Son of the Living God, and that He came into the world to save sinners, which I am. I repent from my old sinful life connected to Satan through my old life in Adam. I renounce my old way of life of putting my trust in myself. I put my trust in your saving grace offered to me through your only Son Jesus Christ. I confess that Jesus is now my Lord and Savior and you are now my heavenly Father forever! I will keep trusting in you until the end. In Jesus name, Amen.

My prayer is that the Almighty God will bless you with the spirit of wisdom and truth that you may come to know Jesus and the hope of His calling and that together we may be brought to maturity concerning the things of God. And God, being the faithful and holy one that He is, will carry this out so that we, the church, will proclaim boldly to the heavens about the manifold wisdom of God.

Read and meditate on the Scriptures below and call on the Lord to be saved:

...if you confess with your mouth that Jesus is Lord and believe in your heart that God raised him from the dead, you will be saved. For with the heart one believes and is justified, and with the mouth one confesses and is saved.

(ROMANS 10:9–10 ESV)

And Peter said to them, "Repent and be baptized every one of you in the name of Jesus Christ for the forgiveness of your sins, and you will receive the gift of the Holy Spirit."

(ACTS 2:38 ESV)

Whether you've just given your life to Christ or if you've just reevaluated your need, trust and believe what God has said in His Word, "that He rewards those who believe that He exists and diligently seek Him!" Read onward and learn how we can allow God to express Himself and His will in and through us, as we turn from worshiping ourselves to worshiping the one true God.

Ponder this:

Could it be any clearer? Our old way of life was nailed to the cross with Christ, a decisive end to that sin-miserable life—no longer at sin's every beck and call! What we believe is this: If we get included in Christ's sin-conquering death, we also get included in his life-saving resurrection. We know that when Jesus was raised from the dead it was a signal of the end of death-as-the-end. Never again will death have the last word. When Jesus died, he took sin down with him, but alive he brings God down to us. From now on, think of it this way: Sin speaks a dead language that means nothing to you; God speaks your mother tongue, and you hang on every word. You are dead to sin and alive to God. That's what Jesus did.

(**ROMANS 6:6–11 THE MESSAGE**)

Discussion:

You used to be dead because of your sins and acts of disobedience. You walked in the ways of the 'olam hazeh (this present age, this world) and obeyed the Ruler of the Powers of the Air, who is still at work among the disobedient. Indeed, we all once lived this way we followed the passions of our old nature and obeyed the wishes of our old nature and our own thoughts. In our natural condition we were headed for God's wrath, just like everyone else.

(**EPHESIANS 2:1–3 CJB**)

As it is written in the above passage, Paul is referring to the past tense, but search yourself and ask: is this still true of you now? Only you and God know the true condition of what you believe about yourself and the state of your eternal salvation, but if you are unsure, I beseech you at this point to ask yourself the following questions:

1. Are you sure of your eternal salvation?
2. In what ways are you still sowing to the field of your old evil sinful nature (living independently of God)?
3. Are you making excuses for the reason why you sin? If so, what is the excuse? Why is that an excuse?
4. Repent and turn to God with your whole heart. Engage your mind in prayer to God, thanking Him for being a Holy God and for His forgiveness and His love for you.

CHAPTER 2

THE PURCHASE

*In him we have redemption through his blood, the forgiveness of
sins, in accordance with the riches of God's grace.*

(EPH. 1:17 CJB)

When my two daughters were young, I used to teach them about
how money works and how to manage it. One of the most fundamental things I taught them about money was the difference between
debit and credit. I taught them that when you buy something in cash or
with a debit card, you're paying for the object in full with money you
already have. Conversely, buying something on credit means we're not
really making a purchase, we're taking out a loan. In order to take a car
home from the lot, get keys to a house, or get a diploma, we have to ask
the bank to make the purchase for us, agreeing that we will pay the bank
back over time until the object or service is fully paid. If, for some reason,
we should miss or refuse payments, the bank has every right to come and
take the object away from us until we pay again. Essentially, when we
borrow money from a bank to buy something, the bank allows us to in
turn borrow the house or car or whatever we have "purchased" until we
can complete the payments in full.

I taught my daughters to abstain from getting a credit card unless absolutely necessary. For any purchase, big or small, it's always better to pay with a debit card or cash because once we make the purchase, that item completely and totally belongs to us. We're free to do with it what we please, and no one will ever have any grounds to take back what we bought.

When we place the human self and its needs as god, as our idol, we treat God as if He is borrowing from the bank of our time, praise, love, money, and so on. We have God on contract, withholding ourselves unless He meets our term guidelines. If He doesn't meet our need in the time and manner that we want, we go and do it ourselves. If we feel like He's not serving us or contributing to our happiness, then we ultimately deem Him unworthy of having us. But the truth is, we are not the ones who purchased God and paid the high price for His soul. In fact, the exact opposite is true. *He*, Jesus Christ, has paid the high price for our lives. He didn't pay in installments. He didn't pay on credit. He paid it all in full up front. If we know this to be true as followers of Christ, why then are we withholding from God what He has already purchased? This isn't just a problem in our walk with Christ, this way of thinking and living is evident in every other area of our lives! We are often so quick and eager to withhold praise, love, generosity, and forgiveness if we get burned by someone or if we don't get what we feel is due to us.

On the flip side of the same coin, some of us feel like God only loans Himself out to those who behave perfectly. We think that if we sin, mishear His calling, or mess up in any way, then He'll come down and take away what He has given us.

We live in constant fear that God does not love us, believing that He is a mean God just waiting for us to mess up. Both of these mindsets are lies that we've been taught at some point in our lives. Those closest to us may loan out their love based on how we perform, which causes us to carry that lie into our relationship with God. But know this in your mind and in your heart: God gave us His best for the payment of our sins. God gave us Jesus. It is finished!

He wiped away the bill of charges against us. Because of the regulations, it stood as a testimony against us; but he removed it by nailing it to the execution-stake (The Cross).

(Colossians 2:14 CJB)

As with a purchase that is truly paid in full, the owner has rights to every part of what he or she purchased. This is how it is with us and God. When He purchased us with the blood of His Son Jesus up on the old rugged cross, He purchased our entire being, spirit, soul, and body. He doesn't pay in installments, paying some now and some later for fragments of who are; He bought us *whole*. You name it—God owns it. Our feelings, our temperament, our body, our mind, our will, our needs—they all belong to Him. When they all belong to Him, He is the one who gets to decide how we use what belongs to Him. When we trust Him in every aspect of our lives, He will provide for our every need:

Think about the ravens! They neither plant nor harvest, they have neither storerooms nor barns, yet God feeds them. You are worth much more than the birds!

(Luke 12:24 CJB)

We become deceived when we think that we only surrender part of our lives to God when we come to know Jesus. Some of us believe the lie and attempt to hold onto complete control of our lives, only opening parts of our lives to God as we are ready. The truth is, when we said "Yes" to God's call to faith, He became our God, our Father, and our Owner—our Life. Because we are wholly His, lacking in no way, we have the grace of God that teaches us to say no to sin and life of the Holy Spirit to lead us in a life obedient to His way of life.

*For when you were slaves of sin, **you were free** in relationship to righteousness; but what benefit did you derive from the things of which **you are now ashamed**? The end result of those things was* *death. However, now, freed from sin and enslaved to God, **you do** **get the benefit it consists in being made holy, set apart for God,** **and its end result is eternal life.***

(ROMANS 6:20–22 CJB)

Christ redeemed us from the curse of the law by becoming a curse *for us for, 'Cursed is everyone who is hanged on a tree' so that in* *Christ Jesus the blessing of Abraham might come to the Gentiles, so* *that we might receive the promised Spirit through faith.*

(GALATIANS 3:13–14 CJB)

The great part about this purchase is that we get a fresh new start with God! Not only does the entirety of our being now belong to the almighty, all-knowing, all-pure God of the universe, we also get a new life, a new self, and new benefits. What belongs to Jesus now belongs to us as well!

…and if we are children, then we are also heirs, heirs of God and *joint-heirs with the Messiah (Christ) provided we are suffering with* *him in order also to be glorified with him.*

(ROMANS 8:17 CJB)

We have been redeemed, purchased back from the father of lies, Satan. He no longer has power over those of us who are children of God. We are free from enslavement to sin and we are now enslaved to righteousness. This was all done for us, through the shed blood of Jesus upon the cross!

To follow after that folly would be to live in accordance with the old, dead evil nature, the sinful person whose life was inherited from Adam. We must trust and believe that we have new life in Christ. We can move on from living for self and trust Jesus to express His life in and through us, thinking more of others than of ourselves. How? With the Holy Spirit leading us in all Truth. From an understanding that the Heavenly Father will richly supply all of His children's needs, we can lead others to rest in

His sufficiency for us, and, indeed, the love we have for one another will prove to the world that we are disciples of Jesus.

Walking forward, we can rest and trust God or continue to entertain the lies of Satan that make us think we alone have the power to meet our needs and not God, a life of rebellion, the old evil nature.

Notice the difference: Satan wants us to think only about ourselves and how we can provide for our own needs. God, however, desires for us to turn away from ourselves and to look to Him, trusting that He will provide for our every need.

Identity Prayer by Dr. Charles Solomon:

Father, thank you for forgiving my sins and taking me out of the life of Adam and grafting me into the life of Christ. Now that I am in Christ, I believe that I was crucified with Him, buried with Him, raised with Him and that I am seated with Him at your right hand. From this moment on, I choose to have your son, Jesus Christ, live His life in me and through me. I consider myself dead to sin and alive to you, and I am counting on the Holy Spirit to make me aware when I forget my death with Christ and try to live His life for Him in my own human wisdom and energy. I will walk in obedience to the Holy Spirit's leading in my life as to present myself to you as an instrument of righteousness, allowing no part of me to be used for sin. Thank you for making Christ and his life real to me. Glorify yourself through me. In Jesus' name I pray. Amen. (https://gracefellowshipinternational.com/resources/wheel-and-line/)

Ponder this:

Satan stole us through his deception at the Fall. We surrendered all our rights to him, and he was our master! When and where did Jesus purchase us? It was when He died on the Cross and rose on the third day. The Bible clearly states that Jesus's death satisfied God's demands of payment for our sins.

*And you, who were dead in your trespasses and the uncircumcision of your flesh, God made alive together with him, having forgiven us all our trespasses, by canceling the record of debt that stood against us with its legal demands. **This he set aside, nailing it to the cross.***

(COL. 2:13–14 CJB)

Old Creation belongs to Satan

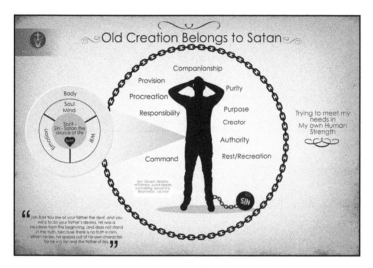

We often forget that at one point, before God opened our eyes to see that we needed a savior, we too were once ones who:

...followed the ways of this world and of the ruler of the kingdom of the air, the spirit who is now at work in those who are disobedient.

(EPH. 2:2 ESV)

God the Father, the one who has purchased us, is a good, *good* Father. He does not use deception or trickery. He gave us His best, Jesus Christ, and asks us to believe in Him. Through this faith in Jesus' death, burial, and resurrection, God purchased us with the blood of Jesus Christ. See the illustration of this truth below:

New Creation belongs to God

Discussion:

We become a child of the greatest being ever, God Himself!

1. In seeing that you are truly God's, how does this change the way you will approach each day?
2. Are you willing to agree with God that every part of your being belongs to Him and that He will take care of your day-to-day needs?
3. Do you live with the mindset that you will be all of God's when you get to heaven?
4. Take a moment and meditate on what it means that God has purchased all of you.

Reflect on the examples of the Old Creation and New Creation.

CHAPTER 3

THE CHANGED MINDSET

I appeal to you therefore, brothers, by the mercies of God, to present your bodies as a living sacrifice, holy and acceptable to God, which is your spiritual worship. Do not be conformed to this world, but be transformed by the renewal of your mind, that by testing you may discern what is the will of God, what is good and acceptable and perfect.

(ROMANS 12:1–2 ESV)

In the last chapter, we discovered that we have been made new in Christ. The old selfish nature has died, and we have been brought into a new life, now in possession of a selfless life from the most selfless person, Jesus. As we prepare to delve into the verse above, and even long after you finish reading this book, keep this essential fact in mind, allowing it to guide your understanding and your behavior:

I appeal to you therefore, brothers, by the mercies of God, to present your bodies as a living sacrifice, holy and acceptable to God, which is your spiritual worship....

(ROMANS 12:1 ESV)

First, we understand that our status of "holy" and "acceptable" is only granted because of God's grace. As Paul implores in the verse, it is by God's mercy that we are counted blameless and holy. By God's grace, we were made righteous. By our faith, we are able to offer ourselves as living sacrifices to God. Keep in mind that being holy and acceptable is what we already are, not what we aim to be. These adjectives, holy, righteous, and acceptable, perfectly describe our nature in Christ.

Do not be conformed to this world....

(ROMANS 12:2A ESV)

It's one thing to understand and accept that we are holy and acceptable, but it's another to take hold of that truth in light of the world around us. The way of thinking in this world will tell us all sorts of lies about how we should be getting our needs met, how we should be living, or how we should be thinking.

The secular mind that is not set upon God will follow secular logic, making decisions based on specific conditions—if this, then that: "If I feel like I'm in a rush, then I will drive irresponsibly," "If someone is rude to me, then I'm going to reciprocate that behavior," or "If my spouse fails to meet my needs, then I will turn to someone else who can." Looking at these thoughts from the world's point of view (remember that Satan is the ruler of this world), these stipulations make perfect sense. With the Fall of man, Satan became the ruler of this fallen world. With Satan at the helm of this world, everything is based solely upon making decision that best fits me—a world of chaos.

But we are not of this world. We no longer follow the logic of this world because it doesn't fit in with who we are in Christ. We who have chosen Jesus Christ now live by faith.

...be transformed by the renewal of your mind....

(ROMANS 12:2B ESV)

This new life of faith is what is meant by "the renewal of your mind." Oftentimes, when we read this opening verse in Romans 12, we misinterpret it to mean that we should try to read the Bible as much as possible. While there is certainly nothing wrong with reading more of God's Word, I think that the renewal of your mind involves more than reading alone.

Why do I think that? Because **James 2:19** tells us that even the demons know God's Word. It is our *faith* in God's Word, though, that separates us from the demons and renews our mind. It is by faith, not by our brute strength and efforts, that we read God's Word and trust Him to keep His promises. He speaks, and we take Him at His word. Faith in action acknowledges the desires that come to mind, takes them captive, and surrenders them to God by faith.

Faith in action trusts God to lead me in behaviors that will glorify God. This is the renewing of the mind, not continuing to walk down the old path that leads to death, but reading God's Word, listening to the Holy Spirit, and trusting God to lead us as we walk in faith. As we do this, instead of traveling down the path of worldly logic to try to obtain a natural desire, we cultivate a habit of faith in God's ability to meet our needs.

...that by testing you may discern what is the will of God, what is good and acceptable and perfect.

(ROMANS 12:2C ESV)

We are then able to test and prove what God's good and perfect will is for our lives. Imagine what we could do with the endless hours we've spent trying to figure out what God's will for our lives. We're searching for deep, complicated answers when God has already told us what His will is for our life.

So they said to him, 'What should we do in order to perform the works of God?' Yeshua (Jesus) answered, 'Here's what the work of God is: to trust in the one he sent!'

(JOHN 6:28–29 CJB)

God's will is only found in faith! Our first and only step is to believe in His son, Jesus. If we focus on our own needs for our life, we'll spend a lot of time trying to figure out our purpose. The focus for seeking God becomes more for self-gratification and not really for God alone. As so clearly stated in the verse above, our faith in Christ automatically puts us in His will!

Throughout life, we live by faith and go where God calls us on the way, knowing that He will provide what we need when we need it. This lifestyle centered on Christ may be completely opposite of what feels or looks good. It may not always be rewarding, and it may not be lucrative. But take heart in this fact: it is a path created by God, and being obedient to God is all that matters!

Ponder this:

And I am sure of this: that the One who began a good work among you will keep it growing until it is completed on the Day of the Messiah Yeshua (Jesus Christ).

(PHILIPPIANS 1:6 CJB)

Discussion:

Stories throughout the Bible demonstrate to us that God's will often runs counter to the worldly way of thinking. Abraham left his country to follow God. He was willing to offer his son Isaac as a sacrifice on an altar to God. The Israelites won battles by blowing horns! Over and over throughout Scripture, we see how God uses "foolish" ways to shame the "wisdom" of this world.

1. Have you ever thought of yourself as holy?
2. If you evaluate your life, would you say that it reflects more of the way of the world or the way of faith?
3. Are you in God's will as described in Romans 12:1, 2?

4. Thank God that He is the one who has started the good work in you and that He will make sure that it is brought to completion.
5. Take a moment and meditate on the fact that God has made you holy and acceptable.

Food for thought:

By faith we understand that the universe was created by the word of God, so that what is seen was not made out of things that are visible.

(HEBREWS 11:3 CJB)

and

But by God's grace I am what I am, and his grace towards me was not in vain; on the contrary, I have worked harder than all of them, although it was not I but the grace of God with me.

(1 CORINTHIANS 15:10 CJB)

CHAPTER 4

THE NEEDS

What agreement has the temple of God with idols? For we are the temple of the living God; as God said, 'I will make my dwelling among them and walk among them, and I will be their God, and they shall be my people.'

(2 CORINTHIANS 6:16 ESV)

There is a law that determines the way almost everything in the universe moves and behaves. Laws of nature tell us how gravity and other forces work; scientific laws show us how atoms fit together to form the world we know. The law of the land determines what is right and wrong for a certain group of people. All of these laws, set in motion by God, the Creator of the universe, regulate our world and dictate how we navigate it. As seen in the above verse, God will make His dwelling among His people and He will be their God, meaning He will care for their every need!

We as humans are no different. We also have needs that govern our lives. I believe that these needs are described in Genesis chapters 1 and 2. Our core needs are for a creator, provision, procreation, responsibility, authority, purpose, source of life, companionship/relationship, rest/recreation, command/order, and purity.

Take, for instance, love, acceptance, worth, and security. These can all be summed up and found in a Godly community/relationship. Within a Godly community/relationship where God is the source and His life is being manifested, one will not only receive but also be a giver of love, acceptance, worth, and security. We see this lived out in the book of Acts.

To function properly, each of us needs to know that each of these desires is met in some way, shape, or form, and how we go about obtaining them is a direct indication of our faith, or lack thereof, in God. Our tactics for getting these needs met reveal what we believe about ourselves concerning God, His Word, and Jesus Christ. It's easy to say that Jesus is the only person who can truly meet all of our core needs, and that is most certainly true and the Biblically sound answer. But if we were to examine our actions, habits, and inner thoughts, what would they say about what we really believe? Disregard a person's words and watch their habits; in their actions, you will learn what they truly believe. God shows us in the book of Isaiah just how much mere flattery pleases Him.

Isaiah wrote:

Then Adonai (Lord) said, "Because these people approach me with empty words, and the honor they bestow on me is mere lip-service; while in fact they have distanced their hearts from me, and their 'fear of me' is just a mitzvah (a precept or commandment: a good deed done from religious duty) of human origin, therefore, I will have to keep shocking these people with astounding and amazing things, until the 'wisdom' of their 'wise ones' vanishes, and the 'discernment' of their 'discerning ones' is hidden away."

(ISAIAH 29:13 CJB)

God had become very disgusted with Israel because they had strayed from worshiping Him with true reverence to mere words of flattery. To the naked eye, they appeared spotless; they spoke the right words and obeyed the traditions that were set before them. But the Spirit searches and knows the heart. The truth is, their hearts were not engaged in the worship of Him, and it was reflected in the way they were living. They were simply going through the motions, and their worship was centered on what felt good to them.

In the passage above, God calls much-needed attention to the lack of faith and reverence in their hearts. His reference to their "hearts" does not refer to their emotions, but to their inner spirit. What God desired was pure reverence to Him, the Great I Am, a Holy God regardless of how fickle the sentiment was. God had clearly taught His people that they were to live a life of fear and respect for Him in everything. This wasn't just for a single generation, but it was also to be taught to their offspring and their offspring's offspring.

Fast forward to the twenty-first century. The Israelites' "lip service" mindset would be the equivalent of our propensity to simply go through the motions today. We watch others and the way they serve God and we settle for simple emulation, so much so that our lives become a series of performative actions with no regard or consideration for truth. The shift today is identical to the Israelites', perfectly fitting to Paul's warning to Timothy about the last days:

> *For the time will come when people will not put up with sound doctrine. Instead, to suit their **own desires**, they will gather around them a great number of teachers to say what their itching ears want to hear.*
>
> (2 TIMOTHY 4:3 NIV)

As Paul states in the verse, our "own desires" have become our focus today, largely because the doctrine of self-centeredness has been passed down through the traditions we've learned. It is no longer about living a life for God, instead, it is all about me. It is about getting my own desires met and about getting God to do things for me and to make me feel a certain way. Self-centeredness often resides as a hidden idol, invisible to one who only listens to the words one speaks. We all have our own learned idiosyncrasies to skillfully mask or hide it, and in some cases, we have entirely forgotten or have never even experienced what is real. We have accepted lies as truth.

> *But understand this, that in the last days there will come times of difficulty. For people will be lovers of self, lovers of money, proud, arrogant, abusive, disobedient to their parents, ungrateful, unholy, heartless, unappeasable, slanderous, without self-control, brutal, not loving good, treacherous, reckless, swollen with conceit, lovers of pleasure rather than lovers of God, having the appearance of godliness, but denying its power. Avoid such people.*
>
> (2 TIMOTHY 3:1–5 ESV)

In Paul's second letter to Timothy, he stressed that being a real Christian in these last days would prove difficult because people would become lovers of themselves and the other things he listed in his letter. If Paul was concerned about the last days in his time, how much more aware, then, should we be hundreds of years later? Yet, instead of becoming more diligent, we have become very lazy in our living. Could it be that we have lost sight of Jesus' sudden return?

Does your life resemble the people Paul mentioned in the verses mentioned above? If so, Paul gives Timothy a clear warning: "Avoid such people." Such are strong words from Paul, but they were written to protect Timothy and those he would eventually choose to be leaders. These are people who would have nothing to do with the truth, even though they have a form of godliness. In the end, it will be revealed that their whole purpose was for selfish ambition. We must be cautious of those who have the form of godliness (piety toward God) but deny the power of godliness! Godliness is a life that reflects the very life of God, and it is a life lived in reverence and respect to the Word of God, a life in the Spirit.

We have many hurts in life. It can become easy to get so caught up in seeking out people who are of like-mindedness amidst the hurts that we lose our true focus on God. Everything that we tend to focus on is around self and what pleases self, and we forget the truth of what God has said in His Word: "Seek first the Kingdom of God and His righteousness" (**Matthew 6:33 ESV**). When we lead with the idol of self, we are seeking the things of God rather than God alone!

The focus of this little book is on that hidden idol we all tend to worship: the self. Throughout this book, we will explore this idol in-depth and how it negatively impacts our lives. Hopefully, by the end, we will be ready to "confess" or agree with God and destroy this idol. You may be thinking, "This book isn't for me! I am not a selfish person!" or you may be on the other end, saying "I know I'm selfish, but it doesn't harm me and I'm getting by just fine." Whichever one you may be, I encourage you to read along and see the truth that God so lovingly gives us in His Word so that you may choose to pursue Him with your whole heart.

I pray that we as a body of believers in Jesus Christ would simply return to our first Love and worship Him in Spirit and in Truth. God knows our motives, and we must be true to what He has spoken through His Word and the Holy Spirit. The thought of a "me first" Christianity is not of God. He has called us to obey Him, for this is a true display of our love toward him. He does not need us to add or take away from what He has said.

> *Whoever has my commands and keeps them is the one who loves me, and the one who loves me will be loved by my Father, and I will love him and reveal myself to him.*
>
> (**JOHN 14:21 CJB**)

Ponder this:

> *Are you tired? Worn out? Burned out on religion? Come to me. Get away with me and you'll recover your life. I'll show you how to take a real rest. Walk with me and work with me—watch how I do it. Learn the unforced rhythms of grace. I won't lay anything heavy or*

ill-fitting on you. Keep company with me and you'll learn to live freely and lightly.

(**Matthew 11:28–30,** *The Message Bible*)

All the ways of a man are pure in his own eyes, but the Lord weighs the spirit.

(**Proverbs 16:2** ESV)

And Samuel said, "Has the Lord as great delight in burnt offerings and sacrifices, as in obeying the voice of the Lord? Behold, to obey is better than sacrifice, and to listen than the fat of rams. For rebellion is as the sin of divination, and presumption is as iniquity and idolatry. Because you have rejected the word of the Lord, he has also rejected you from being king."

(**1 Samuel 15:22–23** ESV)

Discussion:

1. Do you tend to think that you are always right and know best?
2. What is the trigger that causes you to sin against God? Now ask yourself which of the God-given needs you are choosing to not trust God to fulfill.

   For example, when a coworker responds to your input and ideas with disrespect, you respond with anger. The needs you would be trying to fulfill here would be the need for acceptance and authority.

   Confess these to God and choose to accept Him as the source of your authority and respond in love
3. In what ways could you be rebelling against the Lord's command for your life?
4. Repent and take some time to be alone with Jesus. Receive His rest, knowing that He will take care of your every need.

Food for thought:

Moreover, my God will fill every need of yours according to his glorious wealth, in union with the Messiah Yeshua (Christ Jesus). And to God our Father be the glory forever and ever. Amen.

(**PHILIPPIANS 4:19 & 20 CJB**)

and

But seek first his Kingdom and his righteousness, and all these things will be given to you as well.

(**MATTHEW 6:33 CJB**)

SECTION 2

THE IDOL

CHAPTER 5

THE HIDDEN IDOL

...for you shall not worship any other god, for the Lord, whose name is Jealous, is a jealous God.

(EXODUS 34:14 NASB)

Now Rachel had taken the household gods, put them in the saddle of the camel and was sitting on them. Lavan felt all around the tent but did not find them. She said to her father, "Please don't be angry that I'm not getting up in your presence, but it's the time of my period." So he searched, but he didn't find the household gods.

(GENESIS 31:34–35 CJB)

T he word "idol" generally conjures up images in our minds of people worshipping man-made gods. It brings us back to the Old Testament times of golden calves and other false gods that the people of Israel would worship instead of God. But this doesn't apply to us anymore, does it? Nowadays, we no longer bow down to golden bulls or pray to man-made, graven images, so we're good, right?

Wrong!

There is a disguised idol that we all bow to at some point: the idol of "self"—the human self with its God-given needs. Our worship of this false god may not be as explicit or as evident as the Israelites' idolatry throughout the Old Testament, but our tendency to repeatedly worship someone other than the one true God is very clearly revealed when we act out of self-centeredness.

Many of us, like Rachel in the passage from Genesis above, have hidden our idolatry away. We have used the natural aspects of how God created us (for instance, Rachel's menstrual cycle) to try and cover our idolatry up so that others will not know about it. Indeed, now more than ever, the world is run by selfish motives. The word "selfish" is defined in the Merriam Webster dictionary as "concerned excessively or exclusively with oneself; seeking or concentrating on one's own advantage, pleasure, or well-being without regard for others." I would also expand upon the first part of that definition to include such phrases like "concerned excessively or exclusively with *my* people, *my* family, *my* friends, *my* pets, *my* culture, *my* emotions, *my* race, *my* church, my social cause, and so on." The Bible is filled with examples of people living out "selfish" lives, focused solely on self and one's own advantage, pleasure, or well-being, without any regard for God. One such example is Eli and his sons. We read in 1 Samuel how God responds to Eli, who chose to allow his sons to eat the best meat of the sacrifices instead of offering it to God:

> *...why are you showing such disrespect for my sacrifices and offerings, which I ordered to be made at my dwelling? Why do you show more honor to your sons than to me, making yourselves fat with the choicest parts of all the offerings of Israel my people?*
>
> (1 SAMUEL 2:29 CJB)

Like Eli with his sons in 1 Samuel, we show more honor to *my* needs than to God Himself. With that, we have lost reverence and respect for God. We have replaced a concern for the things that God cares about with a concern for ourselves and ourselves alone. We have forgotten what it means to lead a holy life lived in service to a Holy God, for, indeed, God is Holy; and He has called us to be Holy, as He is Holy. But when we center our lives on a "me first" Christianity instead of a complete reverent life devoted to God, it is not pleasing to God; and it becomes increasingly difficult to walk in the holiness He has called us to walk in. "Speak to the entire community of Isra'el; tell them, 'You people are to be holy because I, Adonai (Lord) your God, am holy" **(Leviticus 19:2 CJB)**.

Are we wrong for wanting to care about what is important to us? *No!* God wants us to take care of our family and loved ones. We must, however, watch out for when this care transforms into an idol, when what "I" determine as important becomes such an excessive concern that selfishness dominates every facet of our lives. The obsessive compulsion with what is important to me then becomes the main drive in my life, so much so that I will excuse certain sins (homosexuality, adultery, murder, stealing, lying, etc.) because they hit too close to home, such as when a family member or a close friend is involved. This was the case with Eli. Instead of dealing with the sin of his sons headfirst, Eli looked past it and said nothing. In God's eyes, though, Eli should have handled this situation differently:

> *The sin of these young men was very serious in Adonai's (The Lord's) view, because they treated offerings made to Adonai (The Lord) with contempt.*
>
> **(1 SAMUEL 2:17 CJB)**

Therefore, because of Eli's son's sins, and his lack of honoring God and dealing with them, judgment was brought upon Eli and his two sons. Later in the book, we read about their deaths.

When the unchecked idol of self remains prevalent in our lives, we will always lean toward excusing sinful behaviors in the lives of those we consider important to us. This applies not just to individuals in our lives, but also within groups we value. This is where the idol of self can become especially dangerous because not only does it create its own way to live in our lives, it also embraces others who are creating their own way to live.

They know well enough God's righteous decree that people who do such things deserve to die; yet not only do they keep doing them, but they applaud others who do the same.

(**ROMANS 1:32** CJB)

Oftentimes, those who are living for self will say things like, "That may be true for you, but it's not true for me" or "That was true for them in the Bible, but times have changed." Let us not be fooled, though, for God is the same yesterday, today, and tomorrow:

The Lord is not slow in keeping his promise, as some people think of slowness; on the contrary, he is patient with you; for it is not his purpose that anyone should be destroyed, but that everyone should turn from his sins.

(**2 PETER 3:9** CJB)

James writes in his book of the Bible: "But each person is *tempted* when he is *lured* and *enticed* by his own *desire*"

(**JAMES 1:14** ESV)

In this passage, James is referring to our inward desire to meet our own needs as being greater than the trust we have in God to fulfill His will for our lives. Instead of waiting on God to honor the promises of His Word, we are lured, tempted to seek out another way to meet our own need(s). A few chapters later in James, we read that even when we come before God with requests, we come with selfish motives:

You ask and do not receive, because you ask wrongly, to spend it on your passions.

(**JAMES 4:3** ESV)

James articulates it very clearly—self is the main motive. When we don't get what we have asked from God, we are deceived into bowing down to "self" and say, "I will meet this need of mine." The old lie creeps in and we convince ourselves that God will only help those who help themselves. The truth is, God will help anyone who calls on Him and who will wait on Him.

Selfishness

But if you harbor in your hearts bitter jealousy and selfish ambition, don't boast and attack the truth with lies! This wisdom is not the kind that comes down from above; on the contrary, it is worldly, unspiritual, demonic **(James 3:14-15 CJB)**

Demonic wisdom could be defined as wisdom that is focused on the advancement of self. This is the wisdom that Satan deceived Eve within the Garden, as he said it will make one wise like God so that you will know good and evil. (Genesis 3:4-6)

Selfishness is an expression of the life of Satan, whereas selflessness is an expression of the life of Jesus. Selfishness will always look out for self, even under the guise of helping others, as the end goal is always some type of return. The return can be in the form of hearing a simple "thank you," getting paid, getting some type of acknowledgment, or maybe even hoping God will give me something in return.

One additional reason is that helping others makes us feel good about ourselves! Jesus warned his disciples of this: "But when you give to the needy, do not let your left hand know what your right hand is doing" **(Matthew 6:3 ESV)**. Selfishness will always want to get some type of benefit from what it has done and boast about it. Conversely, God has clearly said, "so that no one should boast before God" **(1 Corinthians 1:29 CJB)**.

We are all born sinners. The very nature of Satan was passed down to us from Adam.

Here is how it works: it was through one individual that sin entered the world, and through sin, death; and in this way death passed through to the whole human race, inasmuch as everyone sinned.

(**ROMANS 5:12 CJB**)

...since all have sinned and come short of earning God's praise.

(**ROMANS 3:23 CJB**)

Because we are all born sinners, we learn how to reason and act from an evil sinful nature. From those sinful beginnings, the numerous misguided individuals surrounding us have taught and even encouraged us toward selfishness. Selfishness is a direct constituent of the one who is the father of selfishness, Satan. A portion of Scripture that we often use to refer to this attribute in reference to Satan is found in **Isaiah**:

You thought to yourself, "I will scale the heavens, I will raise my throne above God's stars. I will sit on the Mount of Assembly far away in the north. I will rise past the tops of the clouds, I will make myself like the Most High."

(**ISAIAH 14:13–14 CJB**)

In these verses, note how the word "I" is used many times, with each proclamation having the sole intention of trying to be like or even above God! This can be traced back to Genesis 3, where Satan deceived Eve by saying "and you will be like God," and from there, the thought of us humans trying to get our natural needs met independently of God with full reliance on self-effort has been passed down to all of us.

We have allowed this self-guided mentality to govern how we live our lives. Some of us may not dare say it, but our actions will show it.

William Ernest Henley famously wrote, "I am the master of my fate, I am the captain of my soul." In more bolder words, this is essentially saying "I will be like God, I am my own god, and I will do whatever it takes to please me and those that I deem important around me!"

A selfless life, however, is the opposite of selfishness.

Selfless

Selflessness is an attribute of our Lord Jesus Christ. A selfless life is one that gives itself away in order to help another without expecting anything in return. It is a life fixed solely on honoring God, with an inherent understanding that God Almighty, the God who created everything, knows how to meet our every need.

The greatest example of a selfless life is found in our Lord Jesus. He taught us how to live a life of selflessness as He trusted the Father to care for His every need. Even when tempted, He still looked to the Father and not His own strength. The Bible states that He became poor that we might become rich **(2 Corinthians 8:9)**. Therefore, through rebirth, He has freed us from the seed of selfishness to live a new life of selflessness, knowing that as we seek the Kingdom of God and His Righteousness, all our needs will be met! (**Matthew 6:33**).

Unfortunately, many of us are like Rachel, who said to Jacob, "Do whatever God has said to do" **(Genesis 31:16 ESV)**. We may publicly acknowledge God to one another, but we will secretly carry a backup plan in our minds just in case God does not move in a way that is favorable for us.

As implied in the title of this book, *Self: The Hidden Idol*, this idol may not arise until we are alone and hidden away from everyone. In isolation, we will dwell on the things we have done, whether good or bad, and set our minds on telling ourselves about how no one acknowledges our efforts. Ultimately, self will always look out for self because it wants to feel important. That was the deception that Satan used on Eve—you are important; you need to look out for yourself rather than trust in God. Satan does not try to get us to focus on Satan or a specific sin, but instead turns our focus inward, illuminating the desire to meet our needs apart from God.

If we would take a closer look at our day-to-day lives, we would see that they are filled with moments where we try to take care of our needs and look out for ourselves, even if it means hurting someone else in the process. Some of the most immediate instances I can think of where this is most evident is when we're traveling and running late or when it is simply a busy time of the year.

We will push, pull, and scream. Maybe some ungodly words will come out of our mouths. We need to ask ourselves—why? Why do we react like this? Is it because someone or something is in our way? Is it because this is hindering us from getting to our destination or from that thing we deem most important? Even if we see a brother or sister in the faith and say, "Calm down, it will be ok," some will be quick to reply, "Don't tell me to calm down; only God understands me right now."

Dare we not say we worship on Sunday in ignorance? Because if we really understood who God is and what He has done for us, we would want to do as Peter advises us:

...but to live such good lives among the pagans (unbelievers) that even though they now speak against you as evil-doers, they will, as a result of seeing your good actions, give glory to God on the Day of his coming.

(1 PETER 2:12 ESV)

Could it be that we have lost sight of these words as we've become caught up in ourselves and what we deem important to us?

The lies are always ever so subtle. As he did with Eve, Satan lures us with counterfeit, fleeting satisfactions of our natural desires. Jesus said, "You shall *love* the Lord your God with all your *heart* and with all your *soul* and with all your *strength* and with all your *mind*, and your *neighbor* as yourself" (**Luke 10:27 ESV**).

"You shall *love* the Lord"—in this instance, the word "love" comes from the Greek word "agapaó." This word is a decisive action word that depicts how God loves us. This type of love is not based on feeling or reward. It simply takes pleasure in doing for the benefit of the other. This love comes from God and is poured into our lives, and this is the only way to have 'agapaó' love back to God. In this passage, we are called to love the Lord with our *heart*, our inner being, the desires guiding our decisions;

with our *soul*, our personality; with our *strength*, our body's power; and with our *mind*, our thoughts and our intellect; and to love our *neighbor*, our community.

Therefore, we can read this passage to say: Take pleasure in the Lord your God with all your inner being, with all the desires guiding your decisions. Take pleasure in the Lord with all your personality. Take pleasure in the Lord with all your body's power. Take pleasure in the Lord with all your thoughts and your intellect. Take pleasure in your community as you would with yourself.

Genesis 18:3–8 is a great example of what it means to delight in the Lord. In this portion of the Bible, Abraham is sitting in the front of his tent, just catching sunrays, when suddenly, the Lord appears before him. Abraham immediately requests that the Lord stay and rest and that God might allow Abraham to wash His feet. Abraham asked nothing for himself. Once the Lord agreed, Abraham went and had his best prepared for the Lord. He found great delight in serving God. In verse 8 (CJB), it says, "And he stood by them under the tree while they ate." He was awestruck and amazed to be able to serve the Lord.

Stop and think. When was the last time you took delight in the Lord? When was the last time you experienced pure pleasure just being in His presence and serving Him?

There is only one God and we are to worship only Him with all that we are because He is the One who created us. Satan's goal is to deceive us into making ourselves our own god, through the *idol of self*. This entails making God out to be a liar that we would ultimately get to decide our own way of living the Christian life. With this faulty thinking, we allow Satan's lie(s) to become truth and the truth of God's Word to become a lie. With Satan's lies leading, our lives may appear as light, but really, they are very dark.

In the upcoming chapters, let's take a closer look at what Jesus encourages us to love and take pleasure in the Lord God, and let's examine how we have been subtly deceived into worshipping the hidden idol of "self." The journey may be painful to handle, but God has made a way out for us to love and take pleasure in Him with our whole being, by His Grace by way of the Cross of Christ.

Ponder this:

One thing have I asked of the Lord, that will I seek after: that I may dwell in the house of the Lord all the days of my life, to gaze upon the beauty of the Lord and to inquire in his temple.

(PSALM 27:4 ESV)

Discussion:

1. What may be some of the ways God has created you that you may use to cover up or make an excuse for being selfish?
2. How are you doing with loving/delighting in the Lord with all your heart, soul, strength, mind, and body?
3. Would a stranger know by your love that you are a disciple of Jesus Christ?
4. Are you a "me first" type of person? Do you think that a "me first" mentality is ok?
5. Take a moment to delight in the Lord alone. Allow this to be a consistent lifestyle change, where you value delighting in God daily.

Food for thought:

...rather, this is happening so that the world may know that I love the Father, and that I do as the Father has commanded me. "Get up! Let's get going!"

(JOHN 14:31 CJB)

and

For God so loved the world that he gave his only and unique Son, so that everyone who trusts in him may have eternal life, instead of being utterly destroyed.

(JOHN 3:16 CJB)

CHAPTER 6

THE HEART

For where your treasure is, there your heart will be also.

(**MATTHEW 6:21**)

T he place in which our treasures lie isn't always self-evident or straightforward. In fact, the paramount spiritual issue for all believers is very often hidden in plain sight: the self. Could it be that our actual treasure is not in Christ but in our own egos? Just as the brain is the control center of the physical body, the heart of man is the true inner self that governs feelings, actions, and motives.

We all tend to make decisions based on how we perceive ourselves. The church we attend, our treatment of others, and whether we love or withhold love—these will all reveal the thoughts we tend to believe about ourselves. Professional counselors, both secular and Christian, will spend most of the counselee's time sifting through their thoughts about "who am I?" The heart of the matter becomes about me, trying to figure out how I became this way or why I did the things I have done—*self!*

For who knows the inner workings of a person except the person's own spirit inside him?

(*1 CORINTHIANS 2:11A CJB*)

If we go back to the beginning of the Bible, after the fall, we see that each person is born with a sinful and wicked heart.

Adonai (The Lord) saw that the people on earth were very wicked, that all the imaginings of their hearts were always of evil only.

(GENESIS 6:5 CJB)

and

The heart is more deceitful than anything else and mortally sick. Who can fathom it?

(JEREMIAH 17:9 CJB)

and

...since all have sinned and come short of earning God's praise.

(ROMANS 3:23 CJB)

Therefore, when we are born, our identity is tied up in this wicked heart, and everything we do stems from its wicked biases. Our upbringing in life started from the foundation of a wicked heart. Almost everything we did came from a wicked state of selfishness. Every hurt that we faced or praise that we received was driven by some form of self. This bred a bend in our identity; we think, "this is just who I am," and we respond to the events of our lives from this erroneous belief about self. It is no surprise that when we come to Christ, we must have our minds renewed from a former way of thinking about who we are; in turn, we will no longer live from a selfish point of view but, by faith, learn to live a selfless life. This only can come about through a crucified life with Christ. Upon the cross the old heart of stone, heart of selfishness, was removed, and we were given a new heart of flesh and of selflessness.

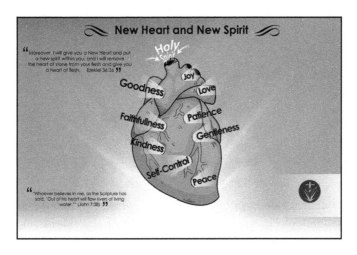

One of the things I often share when speaking is that a "deceived self is a defeated self." A defeated self is one that is defeated in thoughts, defeated in words, defeated in behavior, and defeated in any other area of life. This phrase is especially applicable to those who have accepted Jesus Christ as their Lord and Savior but still live as though the verses mentioned above are speaking about them. Since they still believe that they are wicked, their lives are steeped in shame. Whenever I speak with someone in this position, I always stress that Satan deceived Eve into thinking that God was holding back from her and that they were missing out on something in life—that, basically, both Eve and her husband Adam were incomplete.

Think about this: the two people who were completely perfect and lacked nothing were deceived and found themselves ashamed of who God had created them to be. There was no evil in them, no selfish desires, and nothing about them was bad. They were 100% good!

The lie that Satan told Eve is the very same one that continues to deceive those of us who are in Jesus. We tend to think that we still have a deceitful and wicked heart, but we must reconsider: to think this way is to say that what Jesus accomplished on the cross was in vain! Furthermore, we tend to think that we are not acceptable to God unless we do some type of penitence to get Him to accept us. We forget to thank God for making us holy and acceptable to Him.

> *For in Him all the fullness of Deity dwells in bodily form, and in Him you have been made complete, and He is the head over all rule and authority.*
>
> (COLOSSIANS 2:9–10 NASB)

The Bible clearly tells us that God has poured His love into our hearts:

> *...and hope does not put us to shame, because God's love has been poured into our hearts through the Holy Spirit who has been given to us.*
>
> (ROMANS 5:5 CJB)

We have been circumcised, the cutting away of the wicked sinful nature:

> *Also it was in union with him that you were circumcised with a circumcision not done by human hands, but accomplished by stripping away the old nature's control over the body. In this circumcision done by the Messiah (Christ).*
>
> (COLOSSIANS 2:11 CJB)

And God has removed the heart of stone and given us a new heart:

...and I will give them unity of heart. "I will put a new spirit among you." I will remove from their bodies the hearts of stone and give them hearts of flesh; so that they will live by my regulations, obey my rulings and act by them. Then they will be my people, and I will be their God.

(**Ezekiel 11:19–20** CJB)

Paul encourages us to walk in step with the Spirit because we have been made new:

Since it is through the Spirit that we have Life, let it also be through the Spirit that we order our lives day by day.

(**Galatians 5:24** CJB)

The deceived "self" that is always thinking about self becomes the center of our worship. It rules our judgment and it replaces God as the very center of our lives. When this happens, God is no longer the reason for worship; rather, the reason for worship becomes a perpetual need to discover "what moves me." We pray to the Father, "I want to be in a place that makes me feel..." or "I am looking for a place that meets my needs." Could it be that we have turned away from sound doctrine in our constant pursuit of feeling a certain way?

For the time is coming when people will not have patience for sound teaching, but will cater to their passions and gather around themselves teachers who say whatever their ears itch to hear.

(**2 Timothy 4:3** CJB)

In the last chapter, we saw that Jesus told us to love the Lord God with all our heart. This was not an option; this was a command to obey, without consulting our feelings or perceptions of ourselves. We are able to love God with all of our heart because God has poured His love into our hearts!

Remember, love is an action word! If we are honest, though, we will admit that our standard in Christian conduct revolves around self and not God.

In the opening verse of this chapter, Jesus teaches: "where your treasure is, that is where your heart will be also." Can we truly say that our hearts' treasure is in heaven? Can we truly say that our treasure is Jesus? Or, is our treasure found in my feelings, my earthly desires, and myself, that is, my needs?

Take a long look at yourself and examine your actions. What determines why you do the things you do? The focus should not be on you but on God. If you have been redeemed, then you have a new heart that desires God. Maybe you have been deceived, though, into thinking more about yourself than God and others.

Thoughts of depression, suicide, loneliness, rejection, shame, self-pity, codependency, and many other expressions of despair are focused and fixed on self, and by such thoughts, our false sense of self can lead us down grim, hopeless paths. These paths can be very detrimental and can lead to a very painful end. David wrote:

My spirit faints within me; my heart is appalled within me.

(PSALM 143:4 CJB)

Even the great King David suffered the agonies of self-doubt. David's circumstances overwhelmed his feelings, but David also knew the answer. The answer was not to mope around pitying himself—the answer was to put his trust in God! It is so easy to ruminate on what we feel (or maybe do not feel) emotionally. The saying that "misery loves company" is true.

Satan also knows how to deceive us; he is known as a great deceiver **(Revelation 12:9)**. He doesn't want us to live in freedom and to experience God in every area of our lives. If he can win in the spiritual warfare against destructive self-abasement, not only will he hurt our personal testimony before the world that our God is good, but he will also cause others to doubt God before they ever learn to trust Him.

Our Father God loves us and cares about our every need. Therefore, we can cease worrying about whether our needs will be met. Oh, that we would be like David and put our hope in God when our emotions are going against the truth of what God has said! We would do well to follow David's example of faith in action by worshipping the Lord amidst the lies we may be hearing or telling ourselves.

This, my friend, is to love (take pleasure in) the Lord with all your heart (desire-decisions, your inner self) and to subdue your feelings before Him. When we live in this type of love, Jesus is the one who becomes the source of our desires (true inner self), the one that we take pleasure in. Instead of wallowing in self-centered emotional ups and downs, we turn to God and rejoice that He is the Almighty God. We must choose not to allow our self-seeking desire to determine who we are. Instead, we must choose to set our heart, our desire-decisions, and our affections on the things above where Christ is seated and where we are seated with Him in glory.

Set your affection on things above, not on things on the earth.

(COLOSSIANS 3:2 KJV)

and

...and raised us up with him and seated us with him in the heavenly places in Christ Jesus.

(EPHESIANS 2:6 ESV)

also

*Moreover, it is God who sets both us and you in firm union with the Messiah (Christ); he has anointed us, put his seal on us, and given us his Spirit in our **hearts** as a guarantee for the future.*

(2 CORINTHIANS 1:21–22 CJB)

These verses may sound very superficial, but it is the truth of God's Word and we must take God at His word. If He has said it is so, then no matter what, we must wholeheartedly agree with God. We must believe it in our hearts and confess it with our mouths and then trust that God will save us from the very turmoil that seems to be hindering us in our walk with Him. Say it with me: "my heart is good because God has given me a new heart. He has poured His love into my heart and placed His Spirit in my heart."

Growing up as a child, I had a real identity problem. I was a very shy kid, and because of my shyness, I thought that there was something wrong with me. I spent most of my early life living from the lie that there was something wrong with me and that everyone else knew what I didn't. No matter how hard I worked in school, sports, or life in general, I never felt like it was enough.

Even after becoming a Christian and learning more about God's Word, the lie had stretched so far that I thought God, too, saw something wrong with me. My approach toward God was performance-based, trying to get Him to like me or be pleased with me. I read, I prayed, and I read and prayed even more.

I thought that if I just did more, then perhaps God would look past what I thought was wrong with me, even though I did not know what I thought was wrong with me! This was a complicated problem: because I didn't know what I thought was wrong with me; I had no idea where to even begin fixing what was wrong with me.

Then, one night, God showed me a verse that changed the way I thought about myself. He showed me **1 Corinthians 15:10**: "But by God's grace I am what I am, and his grace towards me was not in vain; on the contrary, I have worked harder than all of them, although it was not I but the grace of God with me." For the first time in my life, I came to understand that God loved me and accepted me just as I was because He had changed me. I was finally able to freely love God with all my heart, without worrying if He accepted me or not because of some deformity I thought was in me.

Living out of a lie can really hurt our walk with God. We must know the truth of God's Word and trust the Holy Spirit to order our lives according to that truth.

Ponder this:

When Christ who is your life appears, then you also will appear with him in glory.

(Colossians 3:4 ESV)

Discussion:

1. What have you allowed to captivate your heart the most?
2. If you have been born again, do you tend to think that you still have a wicked heart? If so why?
3. Accept and confess the truth about what God has said about your new heart in Jesus.
4. Rejoice and thank God for your New Heart!
5. Delight in the Lord with your New Heart which has been filled with the Love of God.

Food for thought:

Who may go up to the mountain of Adonai (Lord)? Who can stand in his holy place? Those with clean hands and pure hearts, who don't make vanities the purpose of their lives or swear oaths just to deceive.

(Psalms 24:3-4 CJB)

and

Therefore, let us approach the Holiest Place with a sincere heart, in the full assurance that comes from trusting—with our hearts sprinkled clean from a bad conscience and our bodies washed with pure water.

(**Hebrews 10:22** CJB)

CHAPTER 7

THE SOUL

And going a little farther, he fell on his face and prayed, saying, "My Father, if it be possible, let this cup pass from me; nevertheless, not as I will, but as you will."

(MATTHEW 26:29 ESV)

We often use the words "heart" and "soul" interchangeably, as if each word has an identical or similar meaning. But Jesus made a clear distinction between the two. He commanded us to "love God with all your heart and all of our soul," clearly distinguishing between "heart" and "soul." As stated in the previous chapter, the heart is who we are at our core. While the heart is primarily what makes us tick, pumping life into the other areas of our human makeup, the soul is the essence of each personality and it should be the expression of our heart. The soul comprised of the emotion, will, and mind

Through the deceitful heart, the emotions, will, and mind were all formed and shaped off of the old nature framework. With this being the case, the way we learn to reason, feel, and think from a child is all shaped incorrectly. We learn to live out of our twisted soul, thinking that my life of who I am is based on how I am feeling or what I am doing which ultimately guides my thinking.

Our soul might also be defined as who we are or how we are perceived by others. The Greek word for soul is "psuché," which we then translate to "psyche," the root word of psychology. If we go back to the heart, the seat of desire-decisions, who we are at our core, we discover that what makes us tick is usually off-center. For our own lives, we too often make choices based primarily on how we feel. In relationships, too, we don't always understand how someone else is feeling because we have not been around that person or we have not talked deeply with them.

The expressions of our feelings can be misguided, perhaps because the heart is hurting or self-deceived. For example, we tend to equate our identity with the work that we do professionally, even when that work does not fully reveal who we really are. If you ask anyone who they are, they will quickly tell you their occupation. The line has become so blurred that simply explaining who we are has become a difficult task. A strong tendency toward self-deception can severely distort our beliefs of who we are, leading us to make choices based on the lies we have heard or the lies we have invented ourselves. We believe the lie and in turn live the lie, even in our Christian walk.

Many of us will say, "I react this way because this is just who I am," maybe even adding, "don't try to change me, because this is who I am." The religious will say, "If God accepts me with my negative attitude, then so should you." However, if we are to live by the truth of the Word of God, then our lives must be radically changed by Jesus Christ, through the power of the Holy Spirit living in us. God's Word instructs us to put to death anything that does not bring God glory:

> *Therefore, put to death the earthly parts of your nature—sexual immorality, impurity, lust, evil desires and greed (which is a form of idolatry); for it is because of these things that God's anger is coming on those who disobey him. True enough, you used to practice these things in the life you once lived; but now, put them all away—anger, exasperation, meanness, slander and obscene talk. Never lie to one another; because you have stripped away the old self, with its ways.*
>
> **(Colossians 3:5–9 CJB)**

When lies have penetrated our belief about who we are, we will excuse our sinful actions by stating, "this is who I am." Even though we often say, "I am a Christian," the unresolved issues of the heart flow out into the soul, causing us to act in ways that do not represent or reflect the new life in Christ Jesus.

Jesus said, "Love God with all your soul." Your soul is your distinct personality. We all have different personalities, but we are to take pleasure in the Lord our God according to the unique expression of our individual personality. If our perceived personality conflicts with the truth, we should take Paul's advice to the Romans:

> *Instead, clothe yourselves with the Lord Yeshua the Messiah (The Lord Jesus Christ); and don't waste your time thinking about how to provide for the sinful desires of your old nature.*
>
> **(ROMANS 13:14 CJB)**

There are many personality tests, and I will not attempt to describe the different personalities defined by those tests here. But whatever your personality is, make the choice to take pleasure in the Lord with all the gifts of your unique personality! Again, this is not an option, this is a command to act by faith. We are to make every effort to rest in the Lord and to walk in His way so that His way becomes our way.

As we obey the truth, which is Christ in us, the Bible tells us that our soul is purified, "Since you have in obedience to the truth purified your souls for a sincere love of the brethren, fervently love one another from the heart" **(1 Peter 1:22 NASB)**. Therefore, as we walk in the truth, we began to see life transformation pumped from our innermost being into the other areas of our lives. Our will, mind, and emotions begin to line up with who we really are.

Jesus was the perfect example of this. While in the Garden of Gethsemane, His soul was in anguish, but Jesus cried out, "not my will but your will be done" **(Luke 22:42 CJB)**. Jesus knew who He was and what His purpose was; therefore, He did not rest in what His emotions were screaming but in the truth of what His Father had said about Him. Jesus was not interested in His own desire to protect and take care of himself; He was only interested in the Father's way. While on the cross in such great physical pain, He cried out and asked the Father to forgive them for they know not what they do!

Jesus could have called down angels to change things, but His own comfort was not His purpose. His purpose was fulfilled in doing the will of the Father.

I can only imagine the pain that He must have felt that night in the garden. In the Gospel of Luke, it states that His sweat was like great drops of blood (**Luke 22:44**). The agony of His soul was so intense that it produced perspiration in the form of blood. Jesus did not win this battle in the garden. This battle was won before it even began, for Jesus said "I know where I come from; and I know where I am going" (**John 8:14**). His choice to obey His Father in all things was His personal victory. It did not rest in "self-will," but in His fixed identity. He knew who He was and what God the Father was doing in His life; and thus, He only did that which pleased the Father, even if it meant giving up His own comfort and pleasure.

If we are in Christ, we, like Jesus, must understand that we have a fixed spiritual identity. We, too, can make the decision ahead of time to go through the pain and agony of the soul with an unshakeable determination and with our eyes upon God, saying, "not my will but your will be done."

My past life does not make me who I am; the cross erased the old and made me new. I am who I am based on what God has done in me and what He has said about me. I will choose to walk in step with the Holy Spirit and allow Him to express the very life of Jesus through my own personality. This is what it means to love the Lord with all your soul—with all your "personality." No one else can love the Lord God the way you can because only you are you!

We must remember that love is not a feeling, but a personal decision. Love is a choice in action. To not love is to not obey, which is sin. The choice is to act in obedience to the Lord's command and to choose the Father's will at all cost.

Ponder this:

And Mary said, "My soul magnifies the Lord, and my spirit rejoices in God my Savior, for he has looked on the humble estate of his servant."

(LUKE 1:46–48 ESV)

Discussion:

1. Are you willing to obey and to love the Lord your God with all your personality?
2. Do you justify the reasons why you do what you do (temperament, character, upbringing, parents, social environment, economic environment, peers, etc.) because you have been taught that it is simply who you are?
3. Are you afraid to allow your "No" to be swallowed up by a "Yes, Lord"? If so, why?
4. Pray about this and let go and trust God. He knows what is best for you.
5. Take the time now to thank God for your personality, and then take a moment to meditate on and Love the Lord with your personality.
6. As you go through your day, allow the Love of God to be expressed through your personality.

Food for thought:

Having purified your souls by your obedience to the truth for a sincere brotherly love, love one another earnestly from a pure heart.

(1 PETER 1:22 ESV)

and

...let the Word of the Messiah (Christ), in all its richness, live in you, as you teach and counsel each other in all wisdom, and as you sing psalms, hymns and spiritual songs with gratitude to God in your hearts. That is, everything you do or say, do in the name of the Lord Yeshua (Lord Jesus), giving thanks through him to God the Father.

(COLOSSIANS 3:16–17 CJB)

CHAPTER 8

THE STRENGTH

Song of Ascents. Of Solomon. Unless the LORD builds the house, those who build it labor in vain. Unless the LORD watches over the city, the watchman stays awake in vain. It is in vain that you rise up early and go late to rest, eating the bread of anxious toil; for he gives to his beloved sleep.

(PSALMS 127:1-2)

As we have seen, if the heart is deceived and primarily set on self, its response to our circumstances will always be based on affections and emotions. This trend also includes our strength, which we exert to do things. Our strength, or our power, can be further defined as how we use our bodies, our words, or our efforts. In our day-to-day lives, we will exert all our energies to accomplish whatever we think is best for us. We take what is felt in the soul, our emotions, and we work toward what gratifies that.

For most Christians, this means trying to work toward righteousness and favor with God by performing "spiritual" actions in our natural capabilities. We think to ourselves, "I must work for God!" But after some months, or even years if you can take it, you'll find yourself burned out, lamenting over the burden you were never meant to carry. Serving, loving, helping, ministering, and living as true disciples of Christ were never meant to be accomplished in our own natural strength; it was meant to be done by His Spirit through us.

Repeatedly throughout the Bible, God demonstrates that anything done apart from Him is done in vain. Everything that God has set aside and planned for us will be accomplished by God regardless of the situation, circumstance, or persons involved, no matter what! Thus, we rest assured that He will give us the strength and ability to accomplish His will. He is the one who gives us what we need, both to rise and labor and to sit and rest. Remember the words in the 23rd Psalm, "He causes me to lie down in green pastures." Those words are not just pretty song lyrics or melodic memory verses, they are the essence of how we should approach life!

Let us not mistake our being "busy" for God with true service. Oftentimes, we think that if we're busy doing something that looks godly, then maybe He'll reward us with something in return. In our efforts to appear holy or to trick ourselves into thinking that our human efforts are pleasing to God, we go for quantity over quality. Ironically though, the Scriptures teach us that we do not owe God anything. Jesus paid the hefty bill for our sin when He died on the cross and rose again to new life! The debt we once owed is now completely forgotten in the sea of God's love. No longer slaves to sin and fear, we are wholly free to love God.

We cannot pay back God for anything that He has done because one, it was a gift, freely given by grace, and two, anything done apart from God, even if it's meant to be for God, is in vain, as it does not please Him. If we could repay God for all that He has done, then salvation wouldn't be a gift, it would be an earned prize. The only thing God requires of us in return is to trust Him and show our love to Him by our obedience to His Word. As a good Father, He will lead us to what He has called us to do and He will then give us the rest we need.

Check out what He has said in His Word:

*He wiped away the bill of charges against us. Because of the regulations, it stood as a testimony against us; but **he removed** it by nailing it to the execution-stake (the cross).*

(**Colossians 2:14 CJB**)

and

Now the account of someone who is working is credited not on the ground of grace but on the ground of what is owed him. However, in the case of one who is not working but rather is trusting in him who makes ungodly people righteous, his trust is credited to him as righteousness.

(**Romans 4:5–6 CJB**)

Does this now mean that we can sit back and do nothing? Absolutely not! It simply means that all my collective efforts and strengths are now focused on that which God has called me to. My labor is unto Him who called me. My motivation shifts from trying to pay God to trusting Him with my life in whichever way He wants. And because of the strength of God that now lives in me as a New Creation, I can perform it wholeheartedly.

What does this mean in practice? Well, Jesus said that we are to love the Lord God with all our strength. This means choosing to love God with every fiber of my being, from the muscles in my face that cause me to smile, to the tongue in my mouth that chooses to respond in love, to the hands that set aside what I want for the sake of others. Love is obedience in action to God's command: love the Lord God with all your strength.

Worshipping the hidden idol begins to creep in when we start to let our emotions motivate how we interact with others. If I don't "feel" happy, then I won't put energy into my face to greet others with cheer. If I don't "feel" loved, then I won't do laundry for a family that doesn't appreciate it. If I don't "feel" like helping, then I'll leave others to their own devices while I go out and "live my best life." The list could go on and on. As an old song would suggest, my life is "my prerogative," I will think and do what I want.

On the other hand, a proper understanding of who we are and whose we are will change how we behave. By God's grace, we are children of the Most High, raised to new life with Jesus and filled with the Holy Spirit, who equips us to walk in accordance with God's will. Because of these fundamental truths, we can now: "For this I toil, struggling with <u>all his energy</u> that he powerfully works within me" **(Colossians 1:29 ESV)**. Even in our labor, there is rest because what we are doing isn't done from strength mustered up apart from God; it is done by the Lord who is working in and through us. "Not by might, but by my spirit says the Lord" **(Zechariah 4:6 ESV)**.

This obedience to God's will in our bodies is not only beneficial for us, but it also displays to others that what we believe is true and trustworthy.

For this is the will of God, that by doing good you should put to silence the ignorance of foolish people.

(1 PETER 2:15 ESV)

When God called me to go and serve on the Navajo Reservation, it meant that I'd be living with a new group of people. I had been there several times on weekly mission trips two years prior to my going to live there full-time. Around my fifth day after moving there, I was attacked by a young man filled with an evil spirit. As I was forced into wrestling with this young man while waiting on the authorities to arrive, I had to keep reminding myself that this young man was not himself. Through the tussle, he bit my arm, busted out my car window with a rock, and threatened both my life and my daughter's life.

While I held him to the ground, listening to his insults and cursing, I just kept praying for him. After he said that he wanted to kill both me and my daughter, I leaned forward and hugged him, saying, "I love you and God loves you." I had come to understand that I did not have to worry about my own life because God had already taken care of that in Jesus. My focus was shifted, instead, on helping this young man by hoping He would experience the Love of God through me.

Ponder this:

But I consider my own life of no importance to me whatsoever, as long as I can finish the course ahead of me, the task I received from the Lord Yeshua (Lord Jesus) to declare in depth the Good News of God's love and kindness.

(Acts 20:22 CJB)

Discussion:

1. Do you tend to think that you must work to prove yourself to God?
2. What does it look like to trust the Lord to labor through you?
3. Do your feelings typically dictate how you respond to people? (Smiling, helping, loving, etc.)
4. Give thanks to God that He has given you the strength to complete what He has called you to do, His life.
5. Take time to meditate on the fact that God has equipped you to Love Him with all of your strength by His Spirit that lives in you.

Food for thought:

*...for it is God who **works in you**, both **to will** and **to work** for his good pleasure.*

(Philippians 2:13 ESV)

Then Samson called to the Lord and said, "O Lord God, please remember me and please strengthen me only this once."

(Judges 16:28a ESV)

CHAPTER 9

THE MIND

But I am afraid that as the serpent deceived Eve by his cunning, your thoughts will be led astray from a sincere and pure devotion to Christ.

(2 CORINTHIANS 11:3 ESV)

The mind is our understanding, our intellect, and our insight—the faculty of our understanding. What are the thoughts that are constantly in your mind? Is your mind dwelling on you, your family, your friends, your money, and what people think about you, or on tomorrow? If we think back to when we first came to know Jesus as our Lord and Savior, God revealed to us that we were awful sinners doomed to hell, but, by the Cross of Christ and by His grace, He saved us. When we entered this new relationship with God, our thoughts became focused on Him and how we could live to please Him. Then, over time, things changed. Old memories somehow found their way back into our minds. Life started happening, as responsibilities with family, work, house, health, and a myriad of other things arose. Slowly but surely, our minds began to drift away from thinking foremost about God to thinking foremost about the things that revolve around self.

A question that would be most indicative of this mindset shift from

God to self is something along the lines of "How can I get God to meet my needs/desires?" I need this house; I want a wife/husband, children, and car, and new job; and I want to grow my church—you name it. With this shift, the focus of our thoughts moved from pure devotion to God to "self-desires."

All the aspects we've mentioned thus far, from the heart to soul, to body, and now to mind, are all interconnected and working together. When one is affected, it affects all the others, which is why it's so crucial we guard our minds against ruminations on "self" above God. For example, when my mind becomes so focused on the cares of this world that it chokes out thoughts of the Word of God, my soul consequently dwindles in passion for worshiping the Lord. My mind's focus on "self" has undergone the "domino effect" to the soul, overriding our heart's focus on God to the point where we cannot even come before the Lord in worship. Before long, it seems that our entire being has become set on trying to get our needs met the best way that we can. We become like Eve, deceived by Satan into thinking that we must look out for ourselves. We have left our pure devotion in and to Christ and replaced it with a defiled devotion:

> *Their worship of me is useless, because they teach man-made rules*
> *as if they were doctrines.*
>
> (MARK 7:7 CJB)

With this defiled devotion, we seek God from a selfish motive, all in hopes of getting ourselves to be "ok." Our motives are now fully led by self:

> *Or you pray and don't receive, because you pray with the wrong*
> *motive, that of wanting to indulge your own desires.*
>
> (JAMES 4:3 CJB)

My self-centered thoughts about God are now revolving around my circumstances and how I am feeling at a certain time. My worship of God loses its sanctity and becomes nothing more than a passed down tradition of man. If I am not feeling it, then I will choose not to think about God. Even if I do think about God, it is still for my glory alone and what He can do for me, rather than simply because of Who He is. My prayer life has now fully become about what's important to self or a thing I know I should do rather than enjoying and delighting in the Lord!

Jesus loved His Father and was constantly thinking about Him. In John 5 and 8, Jesus said, "I only do what I see the Father doing" and "I only speak what I hear the Father saying." Jesus' thoughts were not on Himself and what He was going through, but on the Father, who was with Him always. David wrote, "One thing have I asked of the LORD, that will I seek after: that I may dwell in the house of the LORD all the days of my life, to gaze upon the beauty of the LORD and to inquire in his temple" **(Psalms 27:4)**, and later he wrote, "You have said, 'Seek my face.' My heart says to you, 'Your face, LORD, do I seek'" **(Psalms 27:8)**.

In these passages, David is expressing that love has no motive for itself and that love is solely transfixed on taking pleasure in the Lord. David's sole source of affections was God the Father.

I can remember the first time I read these words. My heart was filled with great joy, and, like David, I sought to fix my thoughts on loving God only. Through the years, God taught me how to do that—through pure devotion to Him. In the mornings, one of the first things I try to do before anything else is to just sit quietly before God. I try not to think about what's going on around me because I know there will be plenty of time for that later in the day, and I allow myself to just sit and think about God. I truly cherish this valuable time in the morning; and I always look forward to starting my day by sitting alone with God, reflecting on Him and who He is.

Later in life, I learned with guidance from others how to keep my mind on God even when I am working hard on something or amidst a trial. This, too, became valuable to me because I began to see that Jesus was desiring to express His life in and through me and that He wanted me to rest upon His sufficiency. Brother Lawrence wrote that one time while he was washing dishes, He saw that it was Christ in Him doing the work.

This was an amazing revelation to me—the simplicity of the Gospel, His life for my life! I began to understand more clearly how to fix my mind entirely on Jesus.

Another simple illustration came when riding in the car with a good friend of mine, Dr. Lewis Gregory. At the time of this car ride, he did not really know me, but we had a few mutual friends and we were all riding to lunch together. During that car ride, it was raining hard. I can remember riding in the back seat and watching as a car pulled out right in front of us in that torrid weather—an initial reaction could have been to panic or maybe even have a response to the other driver. But no, Dr. Gregory responded by proclaiming, "Praise God, thank you Lord." This struck me to my core so much. Dr. Gregory's response initiated my desire to walk with such a conscious awareness of God that my response would be to see Him through every situation. The people we surround ourselves with in our lives should be like Dr. Gregory, inspiring us to glorify God in all that we do. "And they glorified God because of me" **(Galatians 1:24 ESV)**.

Remember, Satan desires to deceive us into thinking that God has left us in the dark about life and that we need to figure it out and take care of ourselves first. With this mindset, the focus is not on Jesus, but on my feelings, my choices, my work, and how to continue to keep myself happy!

But we can live free of a self-centered mindset—this is only possible when we obey Jesus and love the Lord God by taking pleasure in Him with all our minds, all our intellect, and all our understanding. Paul wrote that it is the love of Christ that controls us **(2 Corinthians 5:14)**. The blood of Jesus had affected the way Paul thought, "And as he was saying these things in his defense, Festus said with a loud voice, 'Paul, you are out of your mind; your great learning is driving you out of your mind'" **(Acts 26:24 ESV)**. It was Paul's grasping of the love of God, poured out through the shed blood of Jesus, that changed the way Paul thought.

It is no wonder the Bible tells us to take every thought captive. As we increasingly dwell on a desire/need, we will become overly consumed by it until we find ourselves constantly searching for ways to get this specific need or desire fulfilled. When the solution that is presented does not bring honor to God, we should understand that it exalts itself above the knowledge of God; and therefore, it is to be taken captive. When the thought is one that honors God and seeks His guidance, we are to praise Him.

As I have looked back over my life, I can see that disobedience to God in my decision-making was first established in my thought life. I would occupy myself with a certain need that required arousal in my life, instead of turning to and trusting God for the answer, "In all your ways acknowledge him, and he will make straight your paths" (**Proverbs 3:6 ESV**).

I spent so much time focusing on the desire/need that the more I thought about it, the more it consumed me. Once I became completely obedient to the thought, a solution to get this need met on my terms would present itself. I became so driven by my desires rather than presenting my desires to the Lord and waiting on Him to meet that need.

God has made a way for us to escape this way of thinking. By way of the Cross, we have been set free from the law of sin and death and we are free to love Him with all our intellect, reasoning, thoughts, and anything else you can associate with the mind until every thought that circulates in our mind stems from love to God the Father. This has been made possible by the Blood of Jesus and the guidance of the Holy Spirit. Again, I cannot stress this enough: we were not made to live the Christian life in our own natural human abilities. God has made a way through His son and now His life resides in and through us!

Ponder this:

Now the natural man does not receive the things from the Spirit of God—to him they are nonsense! Moreover, he is unable to grasp them, because they are evaluated through the Spirit. But the person who has the Spirit can evaluate everything, while no one is in a position to evaluate him. For who has known the mind of Adonai (Lord)? Who will counsel him? But we have the mind of the Messiah (Christ)!

(1 CORINTHIANS 2:14–16 CJB)

Discussion:

1. How do you deal with thoughts that come to your mind that don't honor God?
2. Do you think that bad thoughts come from yourself or Satan?
3. Do you think that righteous thoughts come from yourself or God?
4. Why do you think this way?
5. Take time to mediate on God and thank Him for the mind He has given you and to Love Him with your New Mind in Christ.

Food for thought:

Therefore, let anyone who thinks he is standing up be careful not to fall! No temptation has seized you beyond what people normally experience, and God can be trusted not to allow you to be tempted beyond what you can bear. On the contrary, along with the temptation he will also provide the way out, so that you will be able to endure.

(1 CORINTHIANS 10:12–13 CJB)

and

Do not be conformed to this world, but be transformed by the renewal of your mind, that by testing you may discern what is the will of God, what is good and acceptable and perfect.

(ROMANS 12:2 ESV)

THIS IS LIVING

CHAPTER 10

THE STRENGTH TO DO!

I can do all things through Christ who strengthens me.

(PHILIPPIANS 4:13 NKJV)

Contrary to popular belief, this verse in Philippians is not about using Christ for personal benefit or to achieve some personal goal. It isn't about shooting baskets, making touchdowns, finishing school, or anything of that matter. It is about trusting God in every moment, relying on Him for the strength to walk in faith and bring Him glory. Paul had learned what it meant to live both with plenty and with nothing. In his life as a missionary, there were times when support was good and there were times when support was low, but Paul had learned that no matter what, through Christ, he could do whatever God called him to do.

That is why he could write, "I have completed the course that was marked out for me." Even though there were times when things were hard and he wanted to give up **(2 Corinthians 1:8)**, Paul, along with the other Apostles, learned that they could do all things through Christ because they learned that the power was not of themselves but of God.

The illusion of the world is that we must believe in our own abilities to get somewhere in life when, truth be told, we can go wherever God has planned for us in life. He is the one who orders our footsteps. He is the one who directs the path of the righteous. In the end, anything that we gain or accomplish here on earth means nothing if it is not done through Jesus, unto God for His glory, for no human efforts will share in God's glory. That is why Paul wrote:

> *But the things that used to be advantages for me, I have, because of the Messiah (Christ), come to consider a disadvantage. Not only that, but I consider everything a disadvantage in comparison with the supreme value of knowing the Messiah Yeshua (Christ Jesus) as my Lord. It was because of him that I gave up everything and regard it all as garbage, in order to gain the Messiah (Christ) and be found in union with him, not having any righteousness of my own based on legalism, but having that righteousness which comes through the Messiah's (Christ's) faithfulness, the righteousness from God based on trust.*
>
> **(PHILIPPIANS 3:7–9 CJB)**

Paul didn't put confidence in his heritage, his education, his training, or anything that could be credited to himself. Nothing that could have brought praise to man was a concern for Paul. After coming to the knowledge of the Truth, He was only pursuing Christ and what mattered to God. We are not to be deceived into thinking that this world is all there is and that our hope is in vain. We look forward to the coming of our Lord Jesus and to reigning with Him in glory. When God opens the door of blessing for us, we will know that it is of Him and not our own strength. If He has gifted you with a talent or a skill set, then do it unto the Lord. Be cautious and do not allow the gifts He has bestowed upon you to lead you into forsaking the very one who gave you the gift in the first place. When we reach a certain status or accomplishments in life, we cannot then create our own version of the Christian life to fit our new success in life. We don't get the option to tag God or Jesus onto "our" success in life. No, we come to understand that it is only and truly because of Him that I am successful. He could have given anyone else the gifts He has given me.

SELF THE HIDDEN IDOL

Let our lives glorify God, just as we did when we were humble and had nothing. For David wrote:

> *[God,] I have asked two things of you; don't deny them to me as long as I live — keep falsehood and futility far from me, and give me neither poverty nor wealth. Yes, provide just the food I need today; for if I have too much, I might deny you and say, "Who is Adonai?" And if I am poor, I might steal and thus profane the name of my God.*
>
> (**PROVERBS 30:7-9** CJB)

When Jesus was teaching the disciples to pray, He said, "Give us this day our daily bread"

(**MATTHEW 6:11** ESV)

When we have self at the center of attention, we tend to look at what we have or don't have, instead of the One who owns it all. Even when we do come before God to ask for something, we don't get what we ask for because we ask with selfish motives. The problem gets magnified even further when we don't get what we want from God, and so, we go out and try and get it in our own strength. Then, that very thing we wanted so badly becomes such a burden that we either wish we had never had it or try to replace it with something better. It is much better to trust in God because "He knows what we really need."

We see this all too often, though. People start out with very humble beginnings, seeming to have the most sensitive heart for God. Then, one day, they make it to the top and gain riches and the influence of the world. They become deceived by everything around them into living another lifestyle that contradicts the life they once lived. In some cases, they will even create their own distorted me-first Christianity, with the Christian life revolving around how I define it and not what God has written in His Word.

Sadly, the same can also be seen in the person who has nothing. They come to know Jesus, but their worldly possessions and economic status don't see any change. They see that everyone else seems to be doing well, but their lives continue to experience setbacks that prevent them from moving forward. They get frustrated to the point where they want to quit and say, "this Christian life is not for me, I deserve better." They decide to steal, cheat, manipulate, and, even worse, do anything to help them live a better life.

This is not something new to the believers; Asaph wrote:

> *But as for me, I lost my balance, my feet nearly slipped, when I grew envious of the arrogant and saw how the wicked prosper.*
>
> **(PSALMS 73:2-3 CJB)**

I would strongly encourage that you take the time now to read the entire chapter of Psalms 73; it is a great reminder that success is not always good if it is not from God. We are to keep our eyes set on what God has for us and not on anyone else. Jesus said this to Peter after He rose from the dead about his life in comparison to the other disciples:

> *Yeshua (Jesus) said to him, "If I want him to stay on until I come, what is it to you? You, follow me!"*
>
> **(JOHN 21:22 CJB)**

As we obey Jesus and allow the Holy Spirit to lead us, then we can truly say with Paul, "I can do all things through Christ who strengthens me." Why does He give us the strength to do the things He has called us to do? Because it brings glory to the Father in Heaven! In this my Father is glorified that you bear much fruit.

Ponder this:

> *Don't be afraid, for I am with you; don't be distressed, for I am your God. I give you strength, I give you help, I support you with my victorious right hand.*
>
> **(ISAIAH 41:10 CJB)**

So, because you are lukewarm, neither cold nor hot, I will vomit you out of my mouth! For you keep saying, 'I am rich, I have gotten rich, I don't need a thing!' You don't know that you are the one who is wretched, pitiable, poor, blind and naked!

(REVELATION 3:16–17 CJB)

Discussion:

1. Do you approach God as if He is a personal servant or as if He is the Almighty God?
2. How has the world influenced you in your pursuit of life?
3. Would you be satisfied if the only thing God gave you was your daily bread?
4. Can you see how tempting it is to forget or change your belief about God after gaining wealth or becoming poor?
5. Have you become lukewarm in your pursuit of God?

Food for thought:

Dear friends, I urge you as aliens and temporary residents not to give in to the desires of your old nature, which keep warring against you; but to live such good lives among the pagans that even though they now speak against you as evil-doers, they will, as a result of seeing your good actions, give glory to God on the Day of his coming.

(1 PETER 2:11–12 CJB)

CHAPTER 11

THE DENIAL

Then Jesus told his disciples, 'If anyone would come after me, let him deny himself and take up his cross and follow me.'

(MATTHEW 16:24 ESV)

We know that our old self was crucified with him in order that the body of sin might be brought to nothing, so that we would no longer be enslaved to sin.

(ROMANS 6:6 ESV)

As we have been exploring the ways we have been secretly, or maybe even openly, worshipping the idol of "self," we have seen that the Word of God very clearly declares that the selfish life is not of God. At first glance, Jesus' commandment to love the Lord God with all your heart, soul, strength, and mind and to love your neighbor as yourself may seem impossible. Well, that is a true statement! It is impossible to achieve while in a fallen, sinful state—but thank God He had a plan to fix the impossible. After Jesus rose from the grave, He gave power to those who put their faith in Him to live by the life of the Holy Spirit. "Since it is through the Spirit that we have Life, let it also be through the Spirit that we order our lives day by day"(**Galatians 5:24 CJB**).

Sometimes, we run into a problem where we still think we should be carrying our cross. We hear the phrase "I take up my cross daily" often, and, while this sounds very good, has this phrase become just a religious thing we have learned to say ad nauseam? Note that in Luke's Gospel, the word "daily" is there, but it is not in Matthew or Mark. Even so, the point is that when Jesus referred to taking up His cross, He was telling His disciples what was to come with His death and indicating that they would have to do the same. In order to keep following Him, they must deny themselves and take up their cross to go to a place of death. It was not meant that after His death, they would have to keep carrying a cross. That would essentially be saying that His death on the cross was not good enough to satisfy God's demand for the payment of Sin!

It's extremely important to understand that the purpose of the cross was to lead to death. Sin's power was broken in His body (**Romans 6:6**). His blood was shed to forgive us of our sins (**1 John 1:7**). If we are still carrying our cross, then we have not died with Christ. If we have not died with Christ, then we are still stuck in our old sinful state. If we are locked in a never-ending quest to carry our cross and the weight of our sin, it can so easily become an excuse to why we still have the idol of self. Christ's death was in vain and we are still helpless! But no!

In **Romans 6:6**, it states that "our old self was crucified with him." It doesn't say that our old self "is being crucified." It is a done deal. There is no longer a need to carry a cross. The only reason to continue carrying your cross is as we stated in chapter two—if the old, sinful person is still alive. But if you are in Jesus, the Bible clearly states that you have been crucified through Him!

We must know that this is true if we are followers of Jesus. We should be well acquainted with this fact that our old, sinful self has died. Indeed, we have been freed from that old life through the death of our Lord Jesus Christ (**Romans 6:7**)! He did it all for us! That old, sinful person was buried with Christ, and we have been raised to a new life (**Romans 6:8**). This new life is the very life of Jesus—"When the Messiah (Jesus Christ), who is your life, appears, then you too will appear with him in glory!"

(Colossians 3:4). Because the Christian walk is a walk of faith, our faith must be as real to us as the very things we see. We are called to walk by faith and not by sight **(2 Corinthians 5:7)**.

Through this new life in Jesus, we can now fully obey Jesus' command to love the Lord God with all your heart, with all your soul, with all your strength, and with all your mind and to love your neighbor as yourself because He has now equipped us to do so. In the book of Philippians, we read:

> *Do nothing out of rivalry or vanity; but, in humility, regard each other as better than yourselves; look out for each other's interests and not just for your own. Let your attitude toward one another be governed by your being in union with the Messiah Yeshua (Jesus Christ).*
>
> **(PHILIPPIANS 2:3–5 CJB)**

When we are living in union with Christ, we know that our life is no longer our own but that it now belongs to the greatest person ever, God himself! And when we trust Him, as Jesus did, He will see us through everything in life.

As we come to the realization of this amazing truth, we move from a life of living in awareness to self, completely consumed with what is important to self, toward a life of selflessness, a life lived in a loving union with Jesus. When we live this life of selflessness, we are freely able to give of ourselves, knowing that it is God who is at work in and through us. We move from a defeated, deceived self, trying to live life on our own terms because we think God will not meet our needs, to a life of resting in His daily provision of our daily needs. We will be able to stand alongside David and confidently proclaim, "The Lord is my Shepherd and I shall not want" **(Psalms 23:1 ESV)**.

I know this may go completely against what the world teaches or any kind of logic. But that is the essence of what faith is really about, and if it goes against logic, so be it. As it says in **John 3:16**: "For God so loved the world and gave His only begotten son for us sinners"; if we believe that, then we are also called to believe that we died with Him and that we have been raised with Jesus to a new life—the old is gone and the new has come. Let's turn our focus away from the old, sinful self to the righteousness of the *new* redeemed self.

Several years ago, I was called to go into full-time ministry. It was a life that I knew God had called me to live, but I thought that it would be in the Atlanta area. One night while praying, God showed me that my ministry was to serve the Navajo people.

God had me walk away from a nice, well-paying job to go and live completely by faith. He had me give everything away in my house. His words to me were, "You will trust me for everything." Looking at it from a worldly perspective, this really made no sense, but I trusted God and left everything behind by faith.

While living on the Navajo Reservation, we lived in multiple homes and with different people. I have seen God faithfully provide every step of the way. To this day, I have never raised support, but I have always offered my needs up to God and He has met them. It would have been so easy to obsess and worry about my needs, my desires, and my comfort. The thoughts did come up but I learned to just turn those thoughts over to God through prayer and trust Him.

I could have justified giving in to any of these, but it is always better to obey God. Ever since I took that initial step of faith, my thought has always been, "How can I dare compare anything my Master Jesus has asked me to give up with what He gave up for me?"

Ponder this:

But now that you've found you don't have to listen to sin tell you what to do, and have discovered the delight of listening to God telling you, what a surprise! A whole, healed, put-together life right now, with more and more of life on the way! Work hard for sin your whole life and your pension is death. But God's gift is real life, eternal life, delivered by Jesus, our Master.

(**Romans 6:22–23** *The Message*)

Discussion:

1. Are you still carrying your cross? If so, explain why.
2. What are your thoughts about Romans 6:6?
3. Agree with God that you have been freed from sin.
4. Focus on God and pray that He would guide you into the right way of living.
5. Take time to thank God for your co-crucifixion and co-resurrection with Jesus, and now start walking in this new life of freedom.

Food for thought:

For you know how generous our Lord Yeshua the Messiah (Lord Jesus Christ) was for your sakes he impoverished himself, even though he was rich, so that he might make you rich by means of his poverty.

(**2 Corinthians 8:9** CJB)

and

For we who live are always being given over to death for Jesus' sake, so that the life of Jesus also may be manifested in our mortal flesh. So death is at work in us, but life in you.

(**2 Corinthians 4:11–12** ESV)

SECTION 4

FAITH IN ACTION

CHAPTER 12

LOVE YOUR NEIGHBOR
AS YOURSELF

Do nothing from selfish ambition or conceit, but in humility count others more significant than yourselves. Let each of you look not only to his own interests, but also to the interests of others.

(PHILIPPIANS 2:3–4 ESV)

R ecently, my wife and I were on a long train ride in a foreign country after a tiresome, hectic day that concluded a tiresome, hectic week. As we boarded the train, I noticed that my presence in this country where I did not culturally fit in was turning a lot of heads. We found our seats and eagerly plopped down, ready to relax from the day. Before we could get fully settled, an older gentleman got up from his seat without hesitation and came and spoke to us. My lack of understanding of the native language required that my wife translate beside me. He asked a few questions, and my wife answered, but he seemed to be searching for more. The gentleman persisted, asking question after question to the point where it became bothersome to my wife and to the other passengers on the train. Everyone within three rows of where we were sitting could hear what was going on.

As his interrogation continued, and my wife and I began to feel a bit bothered by it, I reminded her and myself amidst the agitation that we will trust God through this and simply be a part of what He's doing. Needless to say, the man continued to inquire about who I was and why I behaved the way I did.

There was no malicious intent in his persistent inquiry, he simply could not understand the joy that radiated from me. Now, this particular train ride took place in an area that heavily frowns upon those who believe in Jesus Christ and who share their faith with others. But I knew what my purpose was. I knew that I had to be obedient to God's calling in that moment and show love to this gentleman, even when I didn't feel like it. I turned to my wife and told her that if he asks me one more time why I am the way I am, I am going to tell him the truth: Jesus Christ. And just like I thought he would, the man was back again, interrogating me with questions. By this time, my wife had left to get water; but thankfully, the young man across from me knew enough English to translate for me in the place of my wife.

In the midst of the crowd, among the several curious passengers who had stood up and were now listening to our conversation, I told the translator to tell the gentleman that the reason why I smile is because of my relationship with Jesus Christ. This seemed to satisfy the gentleman's questions, and he went on his way back to his seat. My interaction with him had ended, but it was just the start for everyone else in earshot.

I went on to explain to the young man who translated for me and to everyone in the crowd around us the entire Gospel. We certainly didn't share the same native tongue, but I believe in the power of the Holy Spirit to open people's ears to hear and understand what they need to.

In our obedience to what God was doing at that moment, everyone around us on the train that day heard the good news about Jesus Christ. If we would have stayed and focused on ourselves and our agitated feelings instead of what God was doing around us, the opportunity to love our neighbor would have been missed.

Looking back on that moment now, I am always reminded that if I had considered my own needs and desires on that train ride, I wouldn't have had the great honor of sharing the living water of Jesus with the two men and the other passengers. This is what the introductory verse of this chapter is talking about—putting others' needs and interests above your own. This is an undeniably hard pill for most to swallow.

What about me and my needs? They matter, right? If I'm busy looking out for others, who will look out for me? If I'm not living for myself, what's the point of living? Our actions are guided by this "You get yours, and I'll get mine" mentality. This is the worldly way of thinking and living. We who have received Jesus as Lord are not of this world; we are of Christ. When we walk in step with the Spirit and allow God's word to work in our hearts, this verse from Philippians becomes the only way we know how to respond.

Jesus instructed us to love our neighbors as ourselves. As we covered before, love is an action that is used to give, not to take. This entails that anything I'm willing to do for myself I'm also willing to do for others, including neighbors, friends, family members, and even my enemies. To truly allow this word to work out in your heart, you must be willing to trust that God really does know the plans that He has for you.

Jesus has never asked us to do something that He would not do Himself; and on top of that, He also gives us the power to complete what He is asking of us. Jesus became flesh, like we are flesh, and died for us so that His Spirit would dwell inside and make us like Him. He did all of this out of trust in the Father's ultimate plan. In fact, the only reason we can even think about becoming the righteousness of God is that Jesus selflessly gave up his place as King and became a servant to love us.

For you know the grace of our Lord Jesus Christ, that though he was rich, yet for your sake he became poor, so that you by his poverty might become rich.

(2 CORINTHIANS 8:9 ESV)

The same love that was graciously displayed on the Cross is the same love that God desires to cultivate in us, His beloved people. God, our Creator and our neighbor, did not withhold His best from us but, instead, offered Him freely. He offered up His only Son, Jesus Christ, so that we may become like Him. Freely we have received, and freely we shall give away. God lavishes His love upon us, and in turn, we lavish our love onto others.

God made this sinless man be a sin offering on our behalf, so that in union with him we might fully share in God's righteousness.
(2 Corinthians 5:21 CJB)

This sincere act of bestowing love upon others is repeatedly exemplified in the book of Acts. After the Holy Spirit empowered the believers in the book of Acts, those who had plenty would give away what they had to those who were in need. It is recorded that they shared everything in common, or what could be called "Community Living" **(Acts 4:32–37)**. Peter, while in Joppa, received a vision from God to go and share the Gospel with people that Peter would consider to be unclean, non-Jewish people, but God showed Peter that He had made them clean and ready to receive the Gospel of Jesus Christ. After the vision, Peter obeyed and went and shared the Gospel with Cornelius and his family and they all received salvation **(Acts 10)**.

Later, we read about Paul and how he put his life on the line for the Gospel. After getting word from the Holy Spirit that His life would be in danger, "except that the Holy Spirit testifies to me in every city that imprisonment and afflictions await me" **(Acts 20:23)**, Paul still was obedient to give of himself and share the Gospel with his neighbor. He made the statement: "But I do not account my life of any value nor as precious to myself, if only I may finish my course and the ministry that I received from the Lord Jesus, to testify to the gospel of the grace of God" **(Acts 20:24)**.

All these examples show us what happened to people who were filled with the Holy Spirit—they were motivated by Love with the understanding that this world was not their home and that God would provide all their needs, and so they trusted God with their possessions and gave of themselves generously.

One of the most quoted Psalms, Psalms 23, declares, "I shall not want." This means that I am not in need, not lacking anything, because the Good Shepherd leads me beside still waters, gives me rest, and knows me intimately. With this principle in mind, we can freely love our neighbors. We can use the very gifts God has given to us to help others come to know God. When we are loving our neighbor as ourselves, we will seek to offer whatever may benefit us to them also.

But sometimes this attitude of generosity doesn't make sense to us. How can I simply give freely to others when I've worked so hard for this myself? Why should I give if I seldom receive praise or thanks for what I do? Consider this, my friend: Jesus endured the same thing. When He walked this earth, He was treated like scum by the very people He came to save. Even though He was seated at the right hand of the Father, He came to earth and dwelled among us to be brutally rejected by those He loved. We must understand this—He was brutally beaten by those He loved. We were His neighbors and because of His love for us and He wants us to share in all of His blessings, He died for us. Because of His love for God and us, He never complained, He never held back His blessings, and He never demanded fair treatment despite His position as the rightful King of Kings. Are we higher than Jesus that we might demand rightful treatment as God's righteous children? By no means!

If the truth be told, this is what we can expect in many ways:

Indeed, all who desire to live a godly life in Christ Jesus will be persecuted, while evil people and impostors will go on from bad to worse, deceiving and being deceived.

(2 TIMOTHY 3:12–13 CJB)

May we be like our Lord, declaring that we do this so that the world may know that we love our Father. May we remain steadfast amidst persecution in our desire to see others enter into this sweet loving relationship with Jesus. At the end of the parable about the Good Samaritan, Jesus had this to say: "Of these three, which one seems to you to have become the 'neighbor' of the man who fell among robbers?" He answered, "The one who showed mercy toward him." Yeshua (Jesus) said to him, "You go and do as he did" **(Luke 10:36 CJB)**.

Let us freely love our neighbor as we would ourselves, not just family, friends, and those whom we deem as important to us, but everyone that God calls our neighbors.

We are free to love others because God has paid the price for us, the cross, to truly live a selfless life and to give His love away.

Ponder this:

For I could wish that I myself were accursed and cut off from Christ for the sake of my brothers, my kinsmen according to the flesh.

(Romans 9:3 CJB)

So from now on, we do not look at anyone from a worldly viewpoint. Even if we once regarded the Messiah (Christ) from a worldly viewpoint, we do so no longer.

(2 Corinthians 5:16 CJB)

And Jesus, looking at him, loved him, and said to him, "You lack one thing: go, sell all that you have and give to the poor, and you will have treasure in heaven; and come, follow me." Disheartened by the saying, he went away sorrowful, for he had great possessions.

(Mark 10:21–22 ESV)

And Zacchaeus stood and said to the Lord, "Behold, Lord, the half of my goods I give to the poor. And if I have defrauded anyone of anything, I restore it fourfold." And Jesus said to him, "Today salvation has come to this house, since he also is a son of Abraham."

(**Luke 19:8–9 ESV**)

In the passages above, we see the rich young ruler and Zacchaeus. They both had plenty in earthly possessions, desired salvation, and knew that Jesus was the answer. One was selfish and put his trust in what He valued, though, while the other put his trust in the only one who could save him—Jesus.

Zacchaeus was quick to point out, "look, you don't have to ask me to give my possessions away, I have already made the choice to do that." This is key: out of his conviction of love for God, Zacchaeus did what was right and holy in the sight of God. Because of this, he heard the words of Jesus, "Salvation has come to this home." As far as the young rich ruler, however, his salvation or security rested in what "he" owned and not the one who created the very things he possessed.

Discussion:

1. What hinders you from loving your neighbor as yourself?
2. Do you have a longing for others around you to be saved and to become a disciple of Jesus Christ?
3. Will you trust God as you step out in faith to love your neighbor as yourself?
4. Which of the two people, the rich young ruler or Zacchaeus, do you tend to mirror?
5. Take time to meditate on what God has done in you through Jesus Christ, and trust Him to express His love to your neighbor the same way He expressed His love to you.

Food for thought:

For although I am a free man, not bound to do anyone's bidding, I have made myself a slave to all in order to win as many people as possible.

(1 Corinthians 9:19 CJB)

and

Do nothing out of rivalry or vanity; but, in humility, regard each other as better than yourselves look out for each other's interests and not just for your own.

(Philippians 2:3-4 CJB)

and

So welcome each other, just as the Messiah (Christ) has welcomed you into God's glory.

(Romans 15:7 CJB)

CHAPTER 13

GOOD INTENTIONS, BUT NOT GOD'S WILL

Then they said, "Come, let us build ourselves a city and a tower with its top in the heavens, and let us make a name for ourselves, lest we be dispersed over the face of the whole earth."...; And the LORD said, "Behold, they are one people, and they have all one language, and this is only the beginning of what they will do. And nothing that they propose to do will now be impossible for them."

(GENESIS 11:4 & 6 ESV)

I remember back in college when I would try to get ahead in class to keep from falling behind. I read the notes, followed instructions to the "t," and meticulously obsessed over every detail. I would finish my work and think to myself, "I've done quite the job! I finished early and finished well!" With great confidence, I turned in the assignment, expecting to hear extensive praise for my academic initiative. I received the exact opposite.

My professor took one look at my work and informed me that what I had done was *not* what he'd asked for. I walked away dejected and defensive. I thought, "Why didn't he just accept the fact that I did a good job and grade me accordingly?" All my hard work on the project had gone to waste, simply because I neglected the most important step: *listening*. Hindsight revealed that I had neglected to listen to what the professor wanted.

There is nothing worse than finding out that you worked hard for hours and hours on end only for it all to be in vain.

This may seem like a silly occurrence that only happens in school or the workplace, but we can all probably relate to this story in one way or another. In fact, this is often the way we live our Christian lives. We work and work tirelessly at different life paths, fooling ourselves into thinking that our worldly ambition and progress is what pleases God. Compliments from peers, praises from the people we admire, and maybe even miracles may confuse us into thinking that we're seeking after the right objectives. Instead of seeking the Kingdom of God and all His righteousness, we try to do it on our own, hoping to be rewarded for our diligence. In the end, we will see that no matter how much work we put in, that is not the path that leads to God. We'll submit our work only to realize we've completely missed the mark!

And then will I declare to them, 'I never knew you; depart from me, you workers of lawlessness.'

(MATTHEW 7:23 ESV)

True godliness has its focus on God, not on self-gratifying personal gain. Are the motives behind your actions based on God's desires? Only you and God know that. But if your life has been built on the lie that working leads to godliness, know and walk in the Truth that God and God alone should be the driving force behind every aspect of our lives. God himself said of the builders of the tower of Babel:

Behold, they are one people, and they have all one language, and this is only the beginning of what they will do. And nothing that **they propose** *to do* **will now be impossible** *for them.*

(GENESIS 11:6 ESV)

The builders had good intentions. They wanted to commune together, build a city, and make a name for themselves by constructing a building that stretched to heaven. On the surface, this would seem like a great and noble thing to do. After all, who wouldn't want to be physically closer to God? But they forgot what God had commanded Adam and Eve from the very beginning:

*Be fruitful and multiply and fill the **earth** and **subdue** it.*

(**GENESIS 1:28**)

Their desires centered on making a name for *themselves* as they worked their way to _heaven. This was not the plan God had for mankind. God intended for humans to fill the *Earth* in order to proclaim *His* name, not ours. Every success, every triumph, and every victory on this Earth is in vain if it isn't done in the name and power of our Lord. We were never meant to work our way into heaven because it simply will not work! There is only one way and that is through His Son, Jesus!

But each one's work will be shown for what it is; the Day will disclose it, because it will be revealed by fire—the fire will test the quality of each one's work. If the work someone has built on the foundation survives, he will receive a reward; if it is burned up, he will have to bear the loss: he will still escape with his life, but it will be like escaping through a fire.

(**1 CORINTHIANS 3:13–15 CJB**)

Our desires to take care of our loved ones and ourselves, to have success in our endeavors, and to live a successful life are not inherently bad, but they must be guided by a trust in God's plan. This will look very different from how the world says things should be done. The world says, "If you don't like the path you're on, create a new one." The world says, "You can be anything you set your mind to." What happens if this new path you want to create is contrary to what God has for you? What happens if the person you want to become is rejecting God's design for your life? We can't go about life simply asking God to bless this or that, as if our selfish ambitions can be granted by the wave of a wand. Look at Jonah, Paul, Peter, even the children of Israel. When guided by their own self-serving objectives, they all ended up in a place where they ultimately had no choice but to call out to God for rescue and guidance.

Even Jesus' life, from a worldly perspective, led to a calamitous ending that didn't benefit Him. He was God's only begotten Son, manifested in the flesh, innocent all His life, but was willing to serve and die for the sinners who so explicitly rejected Him! He was beaten, mocked, spit on, punched in the face, and publicly humiliated by being hung on a cross. If there was anyone who deserved to create a new path and who had the power to do so, it would have been Jesus. But why didn't He? Because He thought not of Himself, but of pleasing the Father and saving the very people whom He created. He selflessly proclaimed:

Not my will but your will must be done.

(LUKE 22:42)

A life spent solely thinking about ourselves hinders our ability to walk in the Spirit and walk in the way Jesus called us: to love others. Love, in its truest form, is something meant to give, not to take, to set others before ourselves. True love carries out these things without expectation of praise or reward.

This is only possible when we truly and consistently renew our minds. Common convention teaches us that if we feel a certain way, then we must act in accordance with that emotion. We say, "I'm feeling like focusing on myself today" or "I've always made time for myself before I make time for others." These mindsets become crutches and coping mechanisms that aren't in line with our new identity in Christ. Instead, we must walk by faith, taking those thoughts captive and surrendering them to God by faith. Our actions are no longer determined by moods and fickle emotions, they are guided by faith, and we can confidently say, "I trust that

God will lead me in actions that will glorify Him and Him alone." As we do so, God will cause our emotions to align with the truth. Emotions are not bad, but they are not intended to be our guide for life—we must give them over to God and trust Him to reveal Himself, even through what is going on with us emotionally.

This is the renewing of the mind: not continuing to walk down a familiar road map, but reading God's Word, listening to the Holy Spirit, and trusting God to create a *new path* for us to travel as we follow His lead. Without faith, it is impossible to please God. Seeking to accomplish something in your own effort for the mere purpose of reputation will never serve you.

> *Then I'll say to myself, "You're a lucky man! You have a big supply of goods laid up that will last many years. Start taking it easy! Eat! Drink! Enjoy yourself!" But God said to him, "You fool! This very night you will die! And the things you prepared—whose will they be?" That's how it is with anyone who stores up wealth for himself without being rich toward God.*
>
> **(LUKE 12:19–21 CJB)**

Doing things in your own human strength is inadequate before God; the only thing that matters before God is faith, for God knows our motives, and if our motive means trusting Him even when it does not feel or even look right, we can rest in the assurance that God will guide us because He is fulfilling His plan. We simply obey and trust. It is not about leaving a legacy or making a name for ourselves or reaching a point where we can enjoy ourselves from our hard labors; our rest is found in Jesus and Jesus is our legacy! The only name that matters is the name that God has said that every knee will bow to, the name that every tongue will confess: Jesus! **(Philippians 2:10–11)**

The best inheritance that we can leave behind for our kids is a life of faith in Jesus Christ. The only words we should concern ourselves with hearing are the words from God, "Well done, my good and faithful servant" (**Matthew 25:21 ESV**). That is the best recognition that we can receive! Author F.B. Meyer once said, "Live deep in God. Do not be dazzled or fascinated by outward things. Be concerned to know God's will and become the organ of His purpose. He will add to you all else that is needful for the fulfillment of your life-course."

> For what will it profit a man if he gains the whole world and forfeits his soul? Or what shall a man give in return for his soul?
>
> (MATTHEW 16:26 ESV)

Ponder this:

> Unless the Lord builds the house, those who build it labor in vain. Unless the Lord watches over the city, the watchman stays awake in vain.
>
> (PSALMS 127:1 ESV)

Discussion:

> All the ways of a man are clean in his own sight, But the Lord weighs the motives.
>
> (PROVERBS 16:2 NASB)

1. Have you been deliberately ignoring the promptings of the Holy Spirit in your life?
2. What are some things that you've gained from compromising in your walk with Jesus?
3. If we believe that God knows everything about our motives, why do you think we still presume we can fool him?
4. Are you living in God's will for your life, or are you living out your dreams and wishes?

5. Take a moment and meditate on the fact that the God who began a good work in you will see it to completion! He will see it to completion!

Food for thought:

Whoever speaks, is to do so as one who is speaking the utterances of God; whoever serves is to do so as one who is serving by the strength which God supplies; so that in all things God may be glorified through Jesus Christ, to whom belongs the glory and dominion forever and ever. Amen.

(1 PETER 4:11 NASB)

CHAPTER 14

Seeing God in and Through Your Circumstances

So Joseph said to his brothers, "Come near to me, please." And
they came near. And he said, "I am your brother, Joseph, whom
you sold into Egypt. And now do not be distressed or angry with
yourselves because you sold me here, for God sent me before you to
preserve life."

(Genesis 45:4–5 ESV)

Early in life, I struggled with resentful feelings toward my father. For years, up until my first daughter was born, I felt like I was cheated of something with my father. I didn't get to enjoy the fulfilling childhood experience that I thought a son should have with his father.

Though I won't expound upon the negative aspects of how my father raised me, know that I struggled with this feeling of resentment toward my father for a long time. As I look back on what I was experiencing at that time, I can't help but notice how much my resentment for my father came from my concerns for myself!

The struggle felt very real because I had made it all about *me*, what *I* thought I should've received, what *I* wanted from my father, and how *I* wanted the relationship to look. I would go to other men for advice wondering what *I* was missing.

Even though I was desperately looking inward, God was using my relationship with my father to graciously teach me more about my relationship with the Heavenly Father. He was showing me how to see Him in every circumstance, no matter how difficult or unfair.

During this extended time of searching, I was reading and learning a lot about God and He was revealing a lot of things about Himself to me. In ignorance, I took this new knowledge and became haughty in it, fulfilling what Paul wrote in **1 Timothy 4:6**: "*he must not be* a recent convert, or he may become puffed up with conceit and fall into the condemnation of the devil."

I certainly wasn't a recent convert, but I was new to learning and studying God's Word. As I grew in knowledge, I fell into the trap of the devil. I became puffed up and conceited with myself, elevating myself over my father and over others and eventually falling into judgment and criticism of other people.

Through time and prayer, God revealed to me that my father imparted to me the love that he knew how to give. God knew who my father would be and how he planned for things to turn out, "For we are his workmanship, created in Christ Jesus for good works, which God prepared beforehand, that we should walk in them" (**Ephesians 2:10 CJB**).

I repented of my ignorant ways and was so thankful to God for showing me that my father was part of His perfect plan all along.

Shortly after that, my very first memory of embracing my father in a hug and saying, "I love you dad," and hearing him say he loved me came to me in my late twenties. He might have said this when I was very young, but I had no memory of that. It felt so awkward yet so real. From that point forward, I was able to freely enjoy my relationship with my father, forgetting what was behind as I turned my focus away from me and what I thought I did not get.

For many years, I had allowed my feelings to fester into a hidden idol in my life—I was worshiping them without even realizing it! Eventually, it got so severe that it hideously manifested itself in my refusal to talk to or respect my father.

The same applies to Joseph's life in the book of Genesis. He had every right to harbor resentment toward his life and at God. At a young age, his mother died while traveling. His father showered him with special treatment because of his birth order, but his prophetic dreams of how others would one day bow to him made his brothers hate him.

Those same brothers grew so jealous of him that they sold him into slavery! They wrongly believed that Joseph controlled how his father loved him or the things that he dreamt of at night. It is so interesting how we can twist a situation back to ourselves, just as Joseph's brothers did. We become jealous of someone when it appears that they have been chosen to receive favor and not us. We become consumed by all these little thoughts: Why not me? Why wasn't I chosen? I wish it could have been me. I deserve it because of who I am. Look at me, I worked just as hard, if not harder than them.

Note here in Joseph's story that his brothers had heard the stories of old. They knew about putting their trust in God and the ramifications of people taking matters into our own hands—they only had to look at their father Jacob and his life with his brother Esau. But instead of learning from their father's life, instead of trusting God through what their baby brother Joseph was saying, they still decided to take matters into their own hands anyway. Like Cain, instead of operating in faith, they operated in *sin*, as sin lay at their door desiring to rule them **(Gen 4:7)**. They did not kill their brother outright, but, in their sinful desire, they certainly wanted to. Instead, they sold him into slavery and he essentially became dead to them because he was no longer there.

After Joseph had arrived in Egypt, he became a very powerful man because God was with him and caused him to prosper. God granted Joseph favor among the Egyptians to the point where he lived in the house of his Egyptian master. However, sometime later, he found himself being mistreated again. Potiphar, who was one of Pharaoh's officials, had a wife who attempted to seduce Joseph, which he rightly rebuffed. Because of Potiphar's wife's selfish desires, because she didn't get what she wanted, she had him thrown in jail. But even when Joseph was in jail, God's favor was still with him. You see, no matter where you are in life, no matter how you got there, when God has you there, He will continue to take care of you. "Yea, though I walk through the valley of the shadow of death… thy rod and staff, they comfort me" (Psalms 23:4).

While in jail, God gave Joseph the interpretation of two dreams for two men that were in jail with him. All Joseph asked was for them to remember him when they got out of jail. When they did eventually get out of jail, one of the men did not remember Joseph. It was only after Pharaoh had a dream and needed someone to interrupt his dream that the other man remembered Joseph, and he told Pharaoh that he knew someone who could interpret his dream. God graciously gave Joseph the ability to interpret Pharaoh's dream, and, from there, he was raised again to a place of power.

Shortly after Joseph had been given power, it could have been so easy for him to just move on with his own life, and, initially, it looked like he did. But God brought the very people who had caused such tremendous pain to Joseph, his brothers who had sold him into slavery, back into Joseph's life. Joseph could have dwelled on his past. He could have thought only about himself and all the horrible things his brothers had done to him. Truthfully, with how much power he had, he could have done whatever he wanted. But Joseph knew that the power that he held was not something he had earned, but something that God had given to him. He understood that his brothers and everyone else who had hurt him had only played their part in God's grand scheme of things. Joseph did not blame them, nor did he blame anyone. Joseph simply saw God in and through everything in his life.

Looking at it from a worldly viewpoint of focusing solely on "me," it would have been logical for Joseph to have some bitter emotions toward his family and all those who caused pain in his life. But no, Joseph only saw God working through all of this. The Bible does not tell us the exact point that Joseph came to this conclusion, but what we see from his life is that no matter where he was, whether at the palace or in prison, Joseph always referenced God as the source of his success and his understanding. What he had learned about God stayed with him and he continued to trust that the one who started the work in him would be the one to bring it to completion **(Philemon 1:6)**. Joseph did not focus on his own needs and desires. He simply trusted that God was at work in His life. No matter what his position was in life, slave, ruler, or falsely accused and in jail, Joseph only saw God!

As believers in God and disciples of Jesus Christ, we must know that no one has control over us. No one can cause anything to happen to us unless God allows it. We must learn to see God in and through all things. No matter how good or bad it gets, it is God who is in control of all things. In the end, the only things that will matter are the things that glorify God. The only way to be sure of this is in Christ, by the life of the Holy Spirit dwelling in us.

When our emotions about "self" become the hidden idol in our lives, the enemy will bring up every injustice from our past against us to try to justify our actions. The enemy does this so that we will agree with his lies and so that we will forget to put our trust in God and worship Him alone. Emotions can be both good and bad, but whenever they become our primary focus, our life and dealings with other people will become just as fleeting as the wind, unaware of which direction they will come from or take us.

The saying "You must have woken up on the wrong side of the bed" will become what we are known for, rather than our love for one another.

This is where resting (abiding) in the vines applies to our lives: "I am the true vine, and my Father is the vinedresser. Every branch in me that does not bear fruit he takes away, and every branch that does bear fruit he prunes, that it may bear more fruit" **(John 15:1–2 CJB)**. As we are in Christ, His life flows through us. His life becomes the source of the fruit that we produce, not our efforts to try and produce fruit for God. The more we learn to rest (abide), the more the Father cleanses and prunes us, therefore causing us to bear more fruit, in which our Father in Heaven is glorified.

Walking in faith is learning to see God in and through everything. It is resting in the fact that this God we say we believe in, who is all knowing, all powerful, and is in control of all things, really is who He says He is!

He does not need our help, but He lovingly allows us to participate in this wonderful life we have in Christ Jesus! Jesus said, "I only do what I see the Father doing and only speak His words" **(John 15:19)**. There is only one life that matters and that is the life of Jesus. He is the only one who lived a perfect and pleasing life before God, and His Resurrection has now given us His very life. We are now a New Creation in Christ Jesus.

Wherever God may be leading you in life, are you willing and ready to go? Are you willing to sit in prison for being falsely accused? Are you willing to dig through chicken poop simply to show the love of Christ? Are you willing to take on abuse and persecution for believing what the Bible says? You fill in the blanks. Each one of us has a different path that we are called to walk.

Some paths will be more glorious than others, but, ultimately, all that matter is that God is glorified in and through our lives. Relying on selfish ambition will not get the words of "Well done, my good and faithful servant," but rather, "Depart from me, you worker of iniquities" **(Matthew 7:23 ESV)**.

Ponder this:

Furthermore, we know that God causes everything to work together for the good of those who love God and are called in accordance with his purpose.

(ROMANS 8:10 CJB)

Discussion:

1. Where do you feel hopeless?
2. In what areas of your life have you given a person power over you?

3. Are you willing to wait on God to manifest His power in your circumstance?

4. Give thanks to God in all things, for this is the will of God (**1 Thessalonians 5:18**).

5. Take a moment and meditate on the fact that if God has brought something hard in your life, He will also give you the grace to get through it, for His grace is sufficient.

Food for thought:

For we do not want you to be unaware, brothers, of the affliction we experienced in Asia. For we were so utterly burdened beyond our strength that we despaired of life itself. Indeed, we felt that we had received the sentence of death. But that was to make us rely not on ourselves but on God who raises the dead. He delivered us from such a deadly peril, and he will deliver us. On him we have set our hope that he will deliver us again.

(2 CORINTHIANS 1:8–10 CJB)

CHAPTER 15

THE HEALING

When Jesus saw him lying there and knew that he had already been
there a long time, he said to him, "Do you want to be healed?"

(JOHN 5:6 ESV)

If you're experiencing life in the same way the man in John 5 was (stuck
in pain and sickness, desperate for spiritual healing, yearning for
answers and freedom from the rut you're in), come to Jesus and find life.
Healing does not lie in an understanding of your past, in any promise
of a better future, or in any forty-step program to a "better life." Healing
comes from Jesus and the finished work of the cross.

I promise you, once you truly understand and grasp that truth, your
life will be changed. This world teaches us that we need to spend hours
upon hours trying to improve ourselves by analyzing the past, over-pre-
paring for the future, and many other tactics, but those of us who know
Christ understand that once we have been purchased, every bit of our life,
past, present, and future, belongs to God. You can analyze all you want,
but the answer, in the end, will always be this: it was all part of God's plan.

We can certainly point fingers and try to identify places in our lives
where Satan was working against us, but Satan can only do what God
allows him to. And not only Satan, but loved ones, strangers, and other

people in our lives have all been a part of God's plan for our lives to bring us to the point where we have no choice but to call out to Him for rescue.

If the old evil nature and everything tied to it have died, why are we still trying to fix it? There is no point in trying to fix what is dead when we have Christ Jesus—the author and perfecter of our faith. All that time we spend living in the past trying to figure out why we are who we are is a waste! There is no need to recreate what happened to our old selves. We must be willing to grow and learn as Paul did, choosing to forget what is behind.

Not that I have already obtained this or am already perfect, but I press on to make it my own, because Christ Jesus has made me his own. Brothers, I do not consider that I have made it my own. But one thing I do: forgetting what lies behind and straining forward to what lies ahead.

(PHILIPPIANS 3:12–13 CJB)

Paul clearly was not living in his past. He knew that there was nothing there for him. When Jesus revealed Himself to Paul, Paul came to understand that He had a new past—the Cross! If anyone could feel miserable about his past, it should have been Paul. His life before Jesus was a life firmly against the very faith which he eventually died for. He watched and approved the stoning of Stephen, and he actively sought to capture and imprison Christians. But as he stated, when God chose to reveal His Son to Him, it changed his life radically! He no longer identified with the old nature, but completely identified with Jesus' death on the cross and His resurrection. He saw and took hold of the fact that God had changed him.

When the Messiah (Christ) was executed on the stake (Cross) as a criminal, I was too; so that my proud ego no longer lives. But the Messiah (Christ) lives in me, and the life I now live in my body I live by the same trusting faithfulness that the Son of God had, who loved me and gave himself up for me.

(GALATIANS 2:20 CJB)

The proud ego that Paul once had died with Christ on the Cross. Note that it is not continually dying, it *died*—past tense, done and over with, no longer and never again operational. Paul goes on to describe the new life with Christ living in him. This is the mystery that Paul spoke about in **Colossians**:

...the mystery hidden for ages and generations but now revealed to his saints. To them God chose to make known how great among the Gentiles are the riches of the glory of this mystery, which is Christ in you, the hope of glory.

(**Colossians 1:26–27** ESV)

Hudson Taylor, the author of *The Great Exchange*, understood what Paul was saying about Jesus—that Jesus exchanged His life for our life, that we might receive new life in Him. This, my friends, is the Truth! We are no longer chained down by our past or any poor decisions that we made in the old evil nature.

When thoughts of the former life arise to try and condemn us, we can always remember the Cross, where we died as well. The truths that we read about in the Bible regarding Paul, Peter, John, and many more are also true of us. The same power that raised Jesus from the grave is now in us, giving us life to live the victorious Christian life!

Moreover, those who belong to the Messiah Yeshua (Jesus Christ) have put their old nature to death on the stake (The Cross), along with its passions and desires.

(**Galatians 5:24** CJB)

This is what Paul had to say to the Romans regarding their new life:

But you, you do not identify with your old nature but with the Spirit—provided the Spirit of God is living inside you, for anyone who doesn't have the Spirit of the Messiah doesn't belong to him.

(**Romans 8:9** CJB)

Are we willing to accept this as true, or will we continue to allow the lies to be our truth, giving ourselves excuses to try and return to the grave to live out of our old evil nature? Because of the Cross, it has been crucified, dead, and buried!

If you are willing to accept the truths that God has spoken over you, then imitate the man that Jesus healed in John 5. Receive healing from your past emotional damage, from your old sinful life, and from anything else holding you back. Walk in the new life of faith Jesus has so freely given you. Those memories of the old can be a reminder of how God has healed you and made you *new*. Peter wrote:

He himself bore our sins in his body on the stake (The Cross), so that we might die to sins and live for righteousness by his wounds you were healed. For you used to be like sheep gone astray, but now you have turned to the Shepherd, who watches over you.
(1 PETER 2:24-25 CJB)

The idol of self will always focus on self and how it can meet its own needs. However, we need to respond to the Lord's voice and get up from worshiping our "self-made" idols to return to worshiping the one true, living God.

Jesus made the way perfectly clear for us when he said, "Come to me!" (Matthew 11:28 ESV) He is the Way, the Truth, and the Life. God has declared: "I AM that I AM" (Exodus 3:14 KJV). See God right now for who He is. See yourself as He has made you. Rejoice in the fact that He has always loved you and that He knows what He is doing with your new life!

We concentrate not on what is seen but on what is not seen, since things seen are temporary, but things not seen are eternal.
(2 CORINTHIANS 4:18 CJB)

Let's repent and say goodbye once and for all to the idol of self, choosing instead to worship God from a pure heart because He has made us clean in Jesus.

The voice spoke to him a second time: "Stop treating as unclean what God has made clean."

(ACTS 10:15 CJB)

When all is said and done, the only things that will matter are those which seek to bring glory to God because He is the Lord God and He will not share His glory or praise with idols such as "self" and "self-effort"!

I pray that we will mature to the point where we can say with Paul, "For me to live is Christ," and say with our Lord Jesus, "Not my will but your will be done" (**Matthew 26:39 ESV**). In this life, amidst suffering, lack of understanding, false accusations, the good times and the bad, and even death, may we confess that my life is yours only and that I was made to glorify you and you alone, God!

Ponder this:

Therefore, if anyone is united with the Messiah (The Christ), he is a new creation—the old has passed; look, what has come is fresh and new!

(2 CORINTHIANS 5:17 CJB)

and

God made this sinless man be a sin offering on our behalf, so that in union with him we might fully share in God's righteousness.

(2 CORINTHIANS 5:21 CJB)

Discussion:

1. Do you need healing?
2. Are you willing to receive God's method of healing for your life— the life of Jesus for your life? Remember the Great *Exchange, His life for our life*!

3. What excuses are you making to avoid walking in the truth of what God has said in His Word?

4. Are you ready to destroy the dead idol of "self" and begin walking in the new "self," with Christ as your life?

5. Take a moment and thank God for Jesus Christ and what He did on the cross for us, and confessed by faith that I am healed!

Food for thought:

Come to me, all of you who are struggling and burdened, and I will give you rest. Take my yoke upon you and learn from me, because I am gentle and humble in heart, and you will find rest for your souls. For my yoke is easy, and my burden is light.

(MATTHEW 11:28–30 CJB)

Epilogue. No More Excuses!

This became known to all, both Jews and Greeks, who lived in Ephesus; and fear fell upon them all and the name of the Lord Jesus was being magnified. Many also of those who had believed kept coming, confessing and disclosing their practices. And many of those who practiced magic brought their books together and began burning them in the sight of everyone.

(Acts 17:17–19a NASB)

On our flight back from China, my wife Shengxi snapped a photo of the earth below us while we were many miles in the air, marveling at the boundless beauty she had just captured. "Oh, how beautiful!" she gushed. We sat there for a few minutes, awestruck at God's beautiful creation and amazed at the enormity of His love for us.

Enjoying God's creation in the simplicity of the plane ride was a simple reminder of what it's like to have unending trust in God. We board an enormous aircraft, trusting the pilot's ability to get us safely to our destination. We trust in this so much that we sleep, watch movies, eat, and drink on the plane, without much regard to the fact that we're many miles above the ground. Even in the midst of turbulence, we continue to trust the pilots to complete the flight. We ride through the bumps, with eyes closed and fully confident in his or her ability to steer and guide the plane.

In our wonderful walk with God, we are called to walk by faith, completely reliant on His sovereign will. We are called to trust that God will get us to our final destination, home with Him! It is not His will that we go through life by way of our own efforts. He wants us to continue to trust Him no matter what, through the beginning, middle, and end. We certainly may experience some turbulence along the way, but we can rest, enjoy, watch movies, eat, and drink, knowing that He has everything under control!

I implore you to hold fast to the trust you have in God and not to rely on your own strength or the strength of this world! Things may be hard, but there will never be a time when you don't need to trust God for your every breath and every step. Know that His plan to conform us to the image of Christ is perfect. Close your eyes and enjoy the ride!

Truthfully, if we are in Christ, the idol of self that we have been talking about is an imposter. Just like the idols of golden calves and pagan statues in the Bible, they were created to try to replace the one true God. You have been told these lies to try to lead you astray from walking in the Truth.

The real you is someone who loves to love God with all your *heart, soul, mind*, and *strength*, and you take great delight in loving your neighbor as yourself. This was made possible when you received Jesus in your life. The time has come where we must destroy the fake idol of self, the lies of Satan that are determined to have you live independently of God.

We must remember that the pain that Jesus went through on the cross, the separation from the Father, giving up heaven to be clothed in sinful human flesh—it was all for us. It was not His sins that Jesus died for, it was yours and mine! He went through all of this for us because He wanted us to enjoy the benefits of being sons and daughters of the Most High God.

Think about it, we were not even born when this happened, but God, the God who created the heavens and the earth, did this so that we could live in a right relationship with Him!

With this understanding, let us make a conscious decision with every moment that we have left here on earth to live out of our new identity because we are a New Creation in Christ Jesus. Jesus has become the new self in us—it is no longer I who live but Christ in me **(Gal. 2:20).**

A New Creation:

Heart: "and hope does not disappoint, because the love of God has been poured out within our hearts through the Holy Spirit who was given to us"

(ROMANS 5:5 NASB)

Soul: "Since you have in obedience to the truth purified your souls for a sincere love of the brethren, fervently love one another from the heart"

(1 PETER 1:22 NASB)

Strength/body: "Or do you not know that your body is a temple of the Holy Spirit who is in you, whom you have from God, and that you are not your own?"

(1 CORINTHIANS 6:19 NASB)

Mind: "For who has known the mind of the Lord, that he will instruct Him? But we have the mind of Christ"

(1 CORINTHIANS 2:16 NASB)

Neighbors: "Beloved, if God so loved us, we also ought to love one another. No one has seen God at any time; if we love one another, God abides in us, and His love is perfected in us. By this we know that we abide in Him and He in us, because He has given us of His Spirit"

(1 JOHN 4:11–13 NASB)

Now that we are a New Creation in Christ Jesus, we must stand on the foundation of His Word lest we allow the false idols of self to make it's way back into our lives: "We are destroying speculations and every *lofty thing* raised up against *the knowledge of God*, and we are taking every thought *captive* to the *obedience of Christ*"

(2 CORINTHIANS 10:5 NASB)

Don't allow the lie to be true...but allow the Truth to be Light!
Don't allow Satan's lies to be True to you... but allow the Truth of God's
Word and the Life of Jesus Christ - Be - have Being, Light - the illumination
for the Path God has called you to walk.

But you, you do not identify with your old nature but with the
Spirit provided the Spirit of God is living inside you, for anyone
who doesn't have the Spirit of the Messiah (Christ) doesn't belong
to him. However, if the Messiah (Christ) is in you, then, on the one
hand, the body is dead because of sin; but, on the other hand, the
Spirit is giving life because God considers you righteous.

(**ROMANS 8:9–10** CJB)

Therefore, if anyone is united with the Messiah (Christ), he is a new
creation—the old has passed; look, what has come is fresh and new!

(**2 CORINTHIANS 5:17** CJB)

Ponder this:

All that awaits me now is the crown of righteousness which the
Lord, "the Righteous Judge," will award to me on that Day—and
not only to me, but also to all who have longed for him to appear.

(**2 TIMOTHY 4:8** CJB)

and

...and since we have a great priest over the house of God, let us
draw near with a true heart in full assurance of faith, with our
hearts sprinkled clean from an evil conscience and our bodies
washed with pure water.

(**HEBREWS 10:21–22** ESV)

Discussion:

1. Are you longing for the coming of our Lord Jesus?
2. Will you choose to stop focusing on what matters to you and focus on what matters to God, knowing that He will take care of you?
3. Reject the desires of the things of this world.
4. Repent and turn from the false worship of self.
5. Take a moment and thank God that through Jesus the false idol of self has been exposed, and now you can freely love the Lord your God with all your heart, soul, mind, and strength, and you can love your neighbor as yourself.
6. Meditate on these truths that you have read, and ask God to fully express His life through you.

Food for thought:

Dear friends, we are God's children now; and it has not yet been made clear what we will become. We do know that when he appears, we will be like him; because we will see him as he really is. And everyone who has this hope in him continues purifying himself, since God is pure.

(1 JOHN 3:2–3 CJB)

and

He who testifies to all these things says it again: "I'm on my way! I'll be there soon!"
Yes! Come, Master Jesus!
The grace of the Master Jesus be with all of you. Oh, Yes!
(REVELATION 22:20:21 *THE MESSAGE*)

God bless you and may we live in this fallen world as New Creations, knowing that this world is not our home and that our Lord Jesus is coming soon! May it be said of you, as it was said about the Thessalonians:

since they themselves keep telling us about the welcome we received from you and how you turned to God from idols, to serve the true God, the one who is alive,

(1 THESSALONIANS 1:9 CJB)

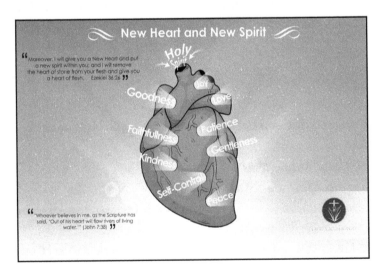

Supplemental Reading "A"

Don't Allow the Lie to Become Truth but Allow the Truth to Be Light!

> You are of your father the devil, and you want to do the desires of your father. He was a murderer from the beginning and does not stand in the truth because there is no truth in him. Whenever he speaks a lie, he speaks from his own nature, for he is a liar and the father of lies.
>
> **(John 8:44 NASB)**

> For God, who said, "Light shall shine out of darkness," is the One who has shone in our hearts to give the Light of the knowledge of the glory of God in the face of Christ.
>
> **(2 Cor. 4:6 NASB)**

> Your word is a lamp to my feet and a light to my path.
>
> **(Ps 119:105 ESV)**

Don't Allow the Lie to Become Truth

The word "lie" is defined in the dictionary as a false statement made with deliberate intent to deceive, an intentional untruth, a falsehood. Most importantly though, a lie is anything that contradicts God's Word or attempts to take it out of context for selfish or condemning purposes. In short, anything that contradicts the Truth is a lie! The Word of God is True, and His Word should be what validates our lives.

As simple as it may seem to identify lies and realize the Truth of God's Word, our circumstances and the lies we're told often cloud our understanding. We hear lies from a very young age in life, and we even tell them from a very young age. We hear things like, "you're ugly," "you're stupid," or "you'll never amount to anything." The list can go on. We hear these things from family members and peers, but mainly from the enemy. These words spoken over our lives often build up a false image of ourselves, and we start living a life based off a lie.

These behavioral patterns based off lies can begin early on in life. If children were to grow up constantly hearing how stupid or worthless they are, then every wrong decision, every misstep in life, and every failed attempt to succeed would be understood as confirmation of those lies. One failed test at school leads them to believe for themselves that they aren't smart. Inevitable blunders in life become reason to believe that their time on Earth is worthless. You see, circumstances begin to feed the lie, and over time, they truly believe that they are stupid and insignificant! As the children get older, they never achieve anything because they honestly believe the lie that they are stupid and worthless. They fear to even try to reach their dreams or chase their goals because the lie has taken control over their lives. They go through life believing that this is who they are!

Many of us have been and are still caught up in these lies that originated from one place: Satan. As seen in John 8:44 and in Revelation 12:9, he is deceiver, and he tells lies. Why? So that we will not be able to accept the true Love of God through Jesus Christ and really experience victory in this life.

How do you continue to live victoriously when there seems to be nothing but darkness in your life? To whom do you run when there is nowhere for you to go? Though it seems like there is no hope, we must believe the Truth! We are never to be the solution! Christ is the only solution that there is for life problems, for God said, "Light shall shine out of darkness." That light is Jesus Christ. The truth as, found in the words of Jesus,

> "I have told you these things, so that in me you may have peace. In this world you will have trouble. But take heart! I have overcome the world"
>
> (JOHN 16:33)

But Allow the Truth to Be Light

The Truth is that the situation is dark, but there is a "light" that can shine very bright in that darkness; that *light* is the Life of Jesus Christ. By the grace of God, we are to learn to see God during and through the darkness, and then you too will be able to say, "Your word is a lamp to my feet and a light to my path."

This is not something to merely conjure up in our thoughts, but by the Holy Spirit, He becomes a guide in their lives. By the power of the Holy Spirit, you'll be able to count it all *joy* and to give thanks to God in all things for this is the will of God! Not in human strength, but by the Spirit of the Lord!

When I minister to the kids on the reservation, I often remind them that even though their situation may be very dark and right now there may not be a way out, they must make the choice to believe what God's word says about them. The Holy Spirit will be the *light* in your life to guide you down the path that God wants you to take because this is the path to which God has called you—it is the only path that will bring Him glory!

> Now this is eternal life: that they know you, the only true God, and Jesus Christ, whom you have sent. I have brought you glory on earth by finishing the work you gave me to do.
>
> (JOHN 17: 3-4)

The Truth is, God's love for us has been poured out, lavishly given, through the shed blood of Jesus Christ. We who were once far off in the world without God have been brought close by the blood of Jesus Christ. All the old lies that we once believed can be put to death at the Cross of Christ.

...fixing our eyes on Jesus, the pioneer and perfecter of faith. For the joy set before him he endured the cross, scorning its shame, and sat down at the right hand of the throne of God. Consider him who endured such opposition from sinners, so that you will not grow weary and lose heart.

(HEBREWS 12:2–3)

We can see that Jesus did it all for us and now He wants to do it all through us. Will we trust Him even though the pain may seem unbearable? My prayer is that we will say "Yes" and that we will encourage one another to say "Yes"!

Because the Truth is that "our present sufferings are not worth comparing with the glory that will be revealed in us"

(ROMANS 8:18)

What lies have you allowed to become truth in your life? Are you willing to take those lies to the cross and allow them to die and to allow God's Truth, Jesus Christ, to be light in your life?

Therefore, if anyone is united with the Messiah, he is a new creation—the old has passed; look, what has come is fresh and new!

(2 CORINTHIANS 5:17)

If *you* are *in* Christ Jesus, the Truth is *you* are a New Creation. Go now, stop living out of the old lies, and *start* living like a New Creation! Don't allow the Lie to become Truth but allow the Truth to be Light!

Supplemental Reading "B"

The Heart!

O ften, we find ourselves praying and asking God to give us a clean heart and renew a right spirit in us because we've rebelled against and grieved the Holy Spirit. The truth is God has already given the believer a clean heart and has given us His Spirit. For those of us who have invited Jesus into our hearts, God has given us the very thing we wanted—a new heart!

When God revealed to us that we were sinners and in need of a Savior, He announced the solution to our problem—His Son Jesus! Upon that old rugged Cross, God prepared a way for our sins to be forgiven and for us to receive a fresh start in life. When this was brought to our attention by the Holy Spirit, we, along with David, cried out to God to create in us a clean heart and renew a right spirit within us

(PSALM 51:10)

Why did we need a New Heart and the Right Spirit with in us?

The heart is more deceitful than all else And is desperately sick; Who can understand it?

(JEREMIAH 17:9)

121

and

For out of the heart come forth wicked thoughts, murder, adultery and other kinds of sexual immorality, theft, lies, slanders…
These are what really make a person unclean.

(MATTHEW 15:19-20A)

Once we said yes to Jesus, something miraculous happened! The wicked and deceitful heart was removed, and we were given a New Heart. Our prayers were answered! This New Heart was not simply an adjustment, an addition, or a patchwork to the old heart. He gave us a New Heart and poured into it His Spirit and Love.

…and hope does not disappoint because the love of God has been poured out within our hearts through the Holy Spirit who was given to us.

(ROMANS 5:5 NASB)

Moreover, I will give you a New Heart and put a new spirit within you; and I will remove the heart of stone from your flesh and give you a heart of flesh.

(EZEKIEL 36:26 NASB)

Since God is Love and has poured His love into our heart, we can therefore be patient, kind, gentle, loving, generous, and the rest of the attributes described in 1 Corinthians 13:4-7. These things are not accomplished by our own efforts, but through God in us! For God, to live is to practice love, patience, kindness, and gentleness, and that life now flows in our hearts and out to others.

Anatomically, the heart pumps blood to the entire body, giving life to its various parts. This is also true of our new spiritual heart—it pumps the life of Jesus to various parts of the body causing us to imitate the life of Jesus. Thus, we see His life flowing in us!

Let's suppose a clot emerges in the veins going down to the legs. It can disrupt blood flow and eventually cause problems for the whole body. The same happens when we choose to rebel and act/live independently of God. This sinful lifestyle is the opposite of who Jesus is in us! We grieve (block the flow of) the Holy Spirit in us, causing us to look like a child of the devil rather than who we really are—a child of God. The Holy Spirit was given to us to empower us to live as children of God in a dark and fallen world.

> Do not grieve the Holy Spirit of God, by whom you were sealed for the day of redemption.
>
> (EPHESIANS 4:30 NASB)

To not love, to not forgive, to hate, to keep a record of someone's else wrong, to not obey, to sin, to be prideful, and to not walk in the Spirit are to walk in rebellion.

> For rebellion is as the sin of witchcraft, and stubbornness is as iniquity and idolatry.
>
> (1 SAMUEL 15:23 KJV)

Because we have a new heart, the Right Spirit in us produces a godly sorrow in us when we have sinned against God. This godly sorrow brings about repentance, or a change from walking in sin and rebellion to walking in obedience. Our repentance allows the Holy Spirit to flow in us, bringing glory to the Father in Heaven who saved us from our sins!

Now, if we find that there is no godly sorrow, no need for repentance within us (self-righteous), then there is a problem—we need to cry out to God to clean our heart and give us the Right Spirit because the wrong spirit (Satan) is producing his life in us!

...the one who practices sin is of the devil; for the devil has sinned from the beginning. The Son of God appeared for this purpose, to destroy the works of the devil.

(1 JOHN 3:8)

Let us not short-circuit the grace of God, but continue to walk in step with the Holy Spirit, allowing the world to see Jesus' life flowing and manifesting itself through us. To God be the glory now and forevermore!

Long after I became a Christian, I thought there was still something wicked in my heart. I cried out to God to create a clean heart in me and to reveal anything wicked in my heart. I implored to God, "I want to desire you and your ways." This went on for a long time until God revealed to me that, surely, He had already given me a New Heart, for my crying out to Him was an expression of my desires for Him!

After placing my trust in the finished work of Jesus' death upon the Cross for my eternal salvation, anytime I made a decision to sin, it was not due to a heart issue but due to my choosing to trust "self" to meet my daily needs. When I did not trust God to meet my needs, I saw myself fixing my focus or thoughts squarely on my desires.

In the book of James, it is written: "Rather, each person is being tempted whenever he is being dragged off and enticed by the bait of his own desire. Then, having conceived, the desire gives birth to sin; and when sin is fully grown, it gives birth to death." It can become so easy to be dragged off by our own inward desires/needs thinking that we must figure out how to satisfy them instead of giving them over to God and waiting on His provision.

Having been enlightened to this truth, I was reminded that God had broken the power of sin in my life on the Cross, so I did not have to give in to the temptation to meet my needs in my own strength. The Holy Spirit revealed that my sins were not originating from a wicked heart, but from my concentrating more on my desires rather than on God, the one who created me with my desires!

All I needed to do was trust God and God alone, the same way I trusted Him for my eternal salvation, by Faith through Grace ("For by grace you have been saved through faith; and that not of yourselves, it is the gift of God" **(Eph 2:8)** and "Therefore as you have received Christ Jesus the Lord, so walk in Him" **(Col. 2:6)**! My heart was already made new. I no longer needed to ask God for something He had already given me through my co-crucifixion and co-resurrection with His Son Jesus Christ ("Being conscious that our old self was put to death on the cross with him" **(Rom 6:6a)** and "Therefore if you have been raised up with Christ" **(Col. 3:1a)**

I received Him by Faith through Grace; therefore I walk in Him by Faith through Grace! As I faithfully trust God to meet my daily needs, Jesus' life living in me becomes supremely evident in my daily walk. My actions began to match my New Life and my New Redeemed Heart as Jesus' life flows to all the other parts of my body!

> Therefore as you have received Christ Jesus the Lord, so walk in Him.
>
> **(Colossians 2:6)**

Thank God for your New Heart, and allow His life to fully flow through you, giving life to your mortal body. Praise God!

> The voice spoke to him a second time: "Stop treating as unclean what God has made clean."
>
> **(Acts 10:16)**

AUTHOR BIO

Willie Smith grew up in a small town called Shiloh, Georgia and is the founder of New Creation517 Inc. He has written several blogs and teaching for his website www.newcreation517.org but Willie never aspired to write a book as he thought there were already enough Christian books on the bookshelves and in people's homes. But being obedient to God, Willie wrote his first book, "Self: The Hidden Idol," a book that concisely demonstrates the ways in which we both actively and passively worship the idol of Self in our lives. Through personal reflection and renouncing of lies that the idol of Self was formulating in his own life, Willie's book teaches on how to replace worship of ourselves with a full understanding of God's grace and the freedom that is found only through the cross of Jesus Christ. Willie remains devoted to sharing the love of God in Jesus Christ along with his wife Shengxi through their ministry as missionaries. In "Self: The Hidden Idol," Willie offers the world what God has taught him, through His Word and by the revelation of the Holy Spirit.